Lorna Doone

by
R. D. Blackmore

adapted by
Berlie Doherty

Resource Material by
Toby Satterthwaite

Series Consultant
Stephen Cockett

Published by Collins Educational, an imprint of HarperCollins*Publishers* Ltd,
77–85 Fulham Palace Road, London W6 8JB

> www.**Collins**Education.com
> On-line support for schools and colleges

© Copyright

First published 2001

ISBN 0 00 330 2261

Berlie Doherty asserts the moral right to be identified as the author of the playscript; Toby Satterthwaite asserts the moral right to be identified as the author of the resource material.

All rights reserved. No part of this publication may be reproduced, stored in a retrieval system, or transmitted in any form or by any means, electronic, mechanical, photocopying, recording or otherwise, without either the prior permission of the Publisher or a licence permitting restricted copying in the United Kingdom issued by the Copyright Licensing Agency Ltd, 90 Tottenham Court Road, London W1P 9HE.

> Photocopying of scripts is illegal. Even if you hold a licence from the Copyright Licensing Agency, this only allows you to copy up to a total of 5% (i.e. one page in twenty) of the whole script.

British Library Cataloguing in Publication Data

A catalogue record for this book is available from the British Library.

Commissioned by Helen Clark, project management by Charles Evans, edited by Angela Wigmore and Charles Evans, picture research by Charles Evans

Design by Nigel Jordan, cover design by Chi Leung, cover illustration by Zhenya Matysiak

Acknowledgements

Illustrations: The Mary Evans Picture Library, p 77, 85; The National Portrait Gallery, p 83; The British Museum, p 84, 88; The British Film Institute, p 91, 92.

Text: Lorna Doone by R. D. Blackmore, Wordsworth Classics, pp 80–81; *The History of England* by Thomas Macaulay, Penguin Classics, pp 86–87.

Whilst every effort has been made both to contact the copyright holders, this has not proved possible in every case.

Production by Katie Morris, printed and bound by Imago in Singapore

For permission to perform this play, please allow plenty of time and contact: Permissions Department, HarperCollins*Publishers*,
77–85 Fulham Palace Road, London W6 8JB. Tel. 0208 741 7070.

> You might also like to visit
> www.**fire**and**water**.co.uk
> The book lover's website

Contents

PLAYSCRIPT

Characters 5

Playscript of *Lorna Doone* 7

RESOURCES

Staging the play 67

Work on and around the script 72

The life and times of R. D. Blackmore 76

From novel to playscript 80

Themes in and around the play 83

Research resources and further reading 96

	Key
71–74	cross-reference between playscript and teaching resources.
71–74	
H	in resources = activity suitable for homework.

Characters

Carver Doone
Lorna Doone (child)
Old John Ridd
John Fry
John Ridd (child)
John Ridd (young adult)
Benita (Italian Lady's maid)
Lorna Doone (young adult)
Lizzie Ridd (John's younger sister)
Annie Ridd (John's older sister)
Mrs. Ridd (John's mother)
Counsellor Doone (old man)
Ridley Doone
Uncle Reuben (old man)
Jeremy Stickles
Judge Jeffreys
Gwenny Carfax (Lorna's maid)
Sir Ensor Doone (old man)
Betty Muxworthy (farm girl)
Tom Faggus (Annie's sweetheart)
Ensie Doone (Carver's son – child)
Boy
King James
Queen
Priest
Commissioner
Doone men, women and children
Farm hands
Servant
Courtiers
Old Lorna Doone

Lorna Doone is set in the wild countryside of Exmoor, between Devon and Somerset. It has several locations and would work without sets or props. Alternatively three acting areas could be designated; one for The Ridd Household, one for The Doone Valley and one for other locations. When Old John is narrating he can wander between locations to link scenes.

The play is in three acts. In act one John and Lorna grow from childhood to adulthood. I suggest that each of these characters is played by three actors; child, young adult, old person. The parts of Lizzie and Annie could be given to two actors. Many of the other parts could be doubled, and there are several very small speaking parts.

Lorna Doone

ACT ONE

Moorland

Music, night. Sound of horses and screaming offstage. **Carver** *strides across the moor track with a richly dressed child (***Lorna***) across his shoulder. She is sobbing. She holds out her hands to a boy (***John***) who is hiding.*

ENTIRE CAST (*enter, making a ring round the tableau, chanting together or variously*)

> And they plunder our farms, they slaughter our cattle.
> They rape our women, they murder our children.
> They kill our menfolk.
> They burn down our homes, they ruin our lives,
> And fill our hearts with terror.
> We will not forgive them.

Lights down.

The Ridd Household

Old John *is sitting at a table, writing with a quill pen.*

OLD JOHN (*reads*) I, John Ridd, of the parish of Oare, in the county of Somerset, (*looking up*) which is as wild and fine a place as any man would hope to see in this world. (*reads*) I, John Ridd, have seen and had a share in some of the doings of this neighbourhood, and will try to set them down. I intend to clear my parish from ill-fame. (*looking up*) I am an ignoramus, but I do pretty well for a yeoman. I want to set down the first time the Doones of Exmoor came into my life. They were as wicked a band of brigands as any I've heard of. They roamed the land as if they owned it. They had their own empire, *Doone Valley*, and from there they ransacked and raped and robbed. Unchecked, because there wasn't a man alive who dared oppose them. They were led by Old Counsellor Doone, Sir Ensor, and Carver.

Counsellor, Sir Ensor and Carver enter.

OLD JOHN There was wickedness in all of them.

Counsellor and Sir Ensor go.

OLD JOHN But the cruellest of all of them was Carver Doone.

Music, as in opening. ***Carver*** *goes.* ***Mrs. Ridd*** *enters with* ***Annie*** *and* ***Lizzie***.

MRS. RIDD And they wrecked the lives of your mother and sisters.

OLD JOHN It was the 29th November, in the year of our Lord Sixteen hundred and seventy three. I will never forget that day, for my life changed in every sense. I was a boy of twelve. I was brought home early from school by our farm-hand, John Fry.

Fry *and* ***Young John*** *enter, moorland.*

JOHN Why hasn't my father come for me?

JOHN FRY Come away home Jan. Tha's needed.

*Briefly lit tableau of **Lady Dugal** with baby, **Benita** with **little Lorna**.*

John And on the way, I see a wealthy woman with her family. The maid talks to me. She is Benita, grand enough to be a lady herself. She is looking after the baby and a pretty little girl. And later that day I see the same little girl being carried away over the moors by a great hulk of a man. The little girl is screaming for help, she holds out her arms to me as if she wants me to save her. Am I sleeping or awake?

*Backlit, **Carver** crosses the track with child **Lorna** flung across his back. She holds out her arms to **John**.*

Old John That image of the little girl holding out her arms for help never left me. And it was the first sight I had of any of the Doones.

Fry Tis Carver Doone. The worst one of them all. The enemy of thy zoul, Jan Ridd.

John Why? What has he done to me?

Fry Come home Jan Ridd. Thy mother needs thee now.

John But the little girl–

Fry I tell thee, come away quick Jan, and save our zouls.

Old John I hurried after him with a strange dread in my heart now, for we had passed the spot where my father always came to meet me, and he was not there.

The Ridd Household

Lizzie *is sobbing.* **Annie** *has her arms round her.*

John *(from outside)* Mother! Father!

Lizzie Tis our John. Who's going to tell him? I daren't.

John runs in, stops, understanding.

Annie Father's dead, John. Killed by the Doones.

John Father! Where's our mother?

Lizzie We don't know. She wouldn't tell us. But we think she's gone to the Doone Valley to speak with their leaders.

They stand with their arms round each other looking across to the Doone Valley.

The Doone Valley

Mrs. Ridd enters. Counsellor, Carver and others are watching her.

Mrs. Ridd (*to audience*) I have never been near this place, nor never wanted to. But I know who I need to speak to, and I try to ignore the coarse stares of these other men.

Carver Doone (*whistles his tuneless signal*) This one's for thee, Counsellor Doone!

Counsellor (*an old man with a very long, grey beard*) Nay, I'm not old enough! I like 'em fresh and raw.

Mrs. Ridd Good sirs–

Carver Sirs, she says? And good. And risking her neck in the Doone Valley to tell us so! Our fame hasn't carried far enough.

Mrs. Ridd I wish to speak to your captain.

Carver Captain? (*shouts*) Ensor! Sir Ensor Doone! Here's a pretty wench come courting you!

The men laugh.

Mrs. Ridd Traitors, murderers, all of you. (***Sir Ensor**, an old, dignified man, comes out*) He is murdered, sir. I have lost the very best husband God ever gave to a woman.

Sir Ensor This matter must be seen to. You may trust the honour of a Doone. If any wrong has been done I will redress it.

Mrs. Ridd Saturday morning I was a wife, sir, and Saturday night a widow, and my children fatherless. There was not a finer man in the whole of Somerset and Devon than my husband, and everybody knows that. He was murdered coming home from Porlock market, with a new gown for me and a shell to put my hair up – oh my good husband!

Sir Ensor Madam, this is a serious thing. My boys are a little wild, I know, and yet I cannot think they would deliberately harm anyone. Counsellor! Over here.

Carver Tis as I said. She's come for thee!

Sir Ensor Counsellor, here is a lady of good repute.

Mrs. Ridd Oh, no sir, only a woman.

Sir Ensor Allow me, madam. Here is a lady of great repute in this part of the country who charges the Doones with having unjustly slain her husband–

Mrs. Ridd Murdered him! Murdered him, if ever there was a murder. Oh sir, you know it! You know it!

Counsellor Put the case.

Sir Ensor The case is this. This lady's husband was slain, it seems, on his way from Porlock market on Saturday night.

Counsellor Cite his name.

Mrs. Ridd Master Ridd. Father of Annie, John and little Eliza, sir.

Sir Ensor Counsellor, we have heard of him often. A worthy, peaceful man, who did not meddle with us. Now, if any of our boys have been rough, they shall pay for it dearly. Yet I can scarcely believe it. People think badly of us, without having any cause to do so. What do you say?

Counsellor Saturday, four or five of our most peaceable gentlemen went to Porlock with a lump of money to buy household goods. On their return a robber of great size and strength attacked them. Carver, our brave and noble Carver, saved the lives of his brothers.

Mrs. Ridd There is no word of truth in this.

Sir Ensor All the Doones are gentlemen. We are always glad to explain, madam, any mistake which the rustic people may make about us. You must be quite clear that we have no intention of charging your husband with robbery. Madam, we will forgive your husband. It is quite likely that he did not know right from wrong at that time of night. The ale is strong at Porlock. *(he hands a pouch to **Ridley Doone**)*

Mrs. Ridd I bid you good day, sir. *(to audience)* Oh no, my pride and my honour will not allow me to stay a moment longer. And when Sir Ensor sends after me with a pouch of money, I throw it at his feet.

All go.

Old John Two years later, I entered the Doone Valley myself. Just by chance I climbed a mighty waterfall. I was fourteen years of age, and young enough to think I could do anything. I fell and thought my knee was broken, and I roared out loud till my mouth was full of water. Then I made up my mind to die.

Young John *lies moaning.* ***Young Lorna*** *approaches and kneels by him.*

Lorna Oh, I'm so glad. Your eyes are open at last.

John I'm not dead?

Lorna Of course not. Now you will try to be better, won't you? What is your name?

John John Ridd, if I'm truly alive.

Lorna And how did you get here, John Ridd? You are soaked to the bone. And what are these wet things in this great bag?

John Leave them alone. They're loaches for my mother. I'll give you some, if you like.

Lorna They're only fish! You do think a lot of them! Look, your feet are bleeding. I must wrap them up for you. Why don't you have any shoes? Is your mother very poor?

John Of course she isn't. We're rich enough to buy this whole meadow, if we wanted to. And here are my shoes in my pocket.

Lorna But they're as wet as your feet! Your poor, bleeding feet! I must do something to help you.

John I'm all right. Why do you keep staring at me like that? And who are you?

Lorna Lorna Doone. Why did you come here? Don't you know what they would do to us if they found you here with me?

John Beat us, I dare say, very hard, or me at least. They could never beat you.

Lorna They would kill us both outright and bury us here by the water; and the river often tells me I must come to that end.

John But why should they kill me?

Lorna Because you have found your way up here, and this is a secret part, and they would never believe it. Please go, oh please go. They will kill us both in a moment.

John But I don't want to go. I like it here. And I like you. Say you like me.

Lorna I like you very much. But you must go.

JOHN Say my name.

LORNA I will call you John if you like. Please go, John. When your feet are better, you can come and tell me how you are.

JOHN I like you very much. Nearly as much as our Annie, and much more than Lizzie. I never saw anyone like you. I must come back tomorrow, and so must you. And I'll bring you so many things – apples, and a thrush I found with a broken leg, and our dog has just had puppies–

LORNA They won't let me have a dog. There isn't a dog in the valley. They say they are such noisy things.

CARVER (*shouts in the distance*) Lorna! Lorna Doone!

LORNA It's Carver! Oh, I'm so afraid of him. (*she clings to him*)

JOHN Then you mustn't stay. Come with me down the waterfall. I can carry you easily, and mother will take care of you.

LORNA Oh, they're here. I can see them.

CARVER (*closer*) Where's the little maid? Lorna?

OTHER VOICES (*offstage*) Lorna Doone, show yourself. Queen! Queen!

CARVER (*offstage, whistles his tuneless notes*) Where the pest is my little queen gone?

LORNA They always call me queen, and I will be their queen one day. Look, there they are by the trees. They're sure to see us now. Hide yourself!

JOHN (*to audience*) She was so afraid that I knew I must do as she told me. So I hid under the water, and nearly got a drowning for it, and they came and carried her off.

OLD JOHN It was seven years before I ventured there again. It was because of my old uncle Reuben that I went, one New Year's Day. I had grown from boy to man in that time.

The Ridd Household

MRS. RIDD (*to audience*) There isn't an ounce of sense in any of them these days. Take that one, for instance. Annie. Just look at her, head in the clouds.

Mrs. Ridd is cooking. **Annie** *setting table.* **Lizzie** *reading.*

MRS. RIDD Why are you so slow today, Annie? You're not with us.

LIZZIE She's mooning, that's what.

MRS. RIDD What's that supposed to mean?

LIZZIE She's seeing stars everywhere she looks, and every one of them has Tom Faggus's face in it.

ANNIE Tis not true. Why should I be interested in Tom Faggus? He's nothing but a common highwayman!

LIZZIE Then why are your cheeks so red, Annie Ridd? I'm right! I'm right!

MRS. RIDD Be quiet you two. All you can do is squabble. What can have kept your Uncle Reuben? John went to look for him an hour ago.

LIZZIE Tom Faggus is very famous, Annie. I shan't mind at all having a highwayman for a brother-in-law.

ANNIE I don't know what you're talking about.

LIZZIE And quite handsome. Not as tall as our John, but quite a man. And he smiles at you so much, and you smile back, I've seen you. Simper, you do. Simper, simper.

ANNIE I don't think I'd know him if I saw him. Tom Faggus?

MRS. RIDD Hush. I can hear them now. Is that your uncle? Oh dear God in heaven, look at the sight of him.

*John comes in half carrying **Uncle Reuben**.*

UNCLE REUBEN (*groaning*) More dead than alive, my dear. Set upon and murdered in the dark.

MRS. RIDD Who did this to you? They've knocked the wind out of you, whoever they be. Let me help you to the sofa.

JOHN I found him tied back to front on a wild pony.

UNCLE REUBEN Stole my money and my horse and my life, they did. Killed me on New Year's day.

MRS. RIDD Hush now. Help me with him, Annie. Lizzie, get hot water and ointments, and we'll put him right. You must thank God that you've never been robbed before in spite of living so long in the world. There, they have torn your shirt, and it is easy to see your wounds aren't mortal, and easy for me to get at them and wash them. Thank the lord for that, too. Get a bed prepared, girls.

***Annie** and **Lizzie** go.*

JOHN Who did it, uncle. Do you know?

UNCLE REUBEN Of course I know, and so would any fool. The Doones did it. Have you ever been into the Doone Valley, John?

JOHN I did once. Seven years ago.

UNCLE REUBEN It could be taken in half an hour by a giant like you and a handful of strong men. Think on it. Go and look again. We must get rid of these murderers somehow.

***Uncle Reuben**, **Mrs. Ridd** and **Young John** go.*

OLD JOHN And so I did go again, but it was not revenge I had in mind. I remembered the child I had met there long ago. And I a man of twenty, went kitted out in a brand new suit on Saint Valentine's Day – to climb a mountain in! No, I had not forgotten her.

The Doone Valley

Bathed in Spring sunlight.

Lorna I watch out for him, hoping against hope that he isn't just a dream. When I see him coming, I want to run into his arms. But I'm a young lady now. Fourteen.

John enters. She stands and watches.

John Lorna Doone!

Lorna Oh, indeed! And if you please, who are you, sir, and how do you know my name?

John I am John Ridd. The boy who gave you those beautiful fish, when you were only a little thing, seven years ago today.

Lorna Yes, the poor boy who was so frightened, and hid himself in the water.

John Do you remember how kind you were, and saved my life by your quickness, and went away riding on a great man's shoulders as if you had never seen me, and yet looked back at me through the willow trees?

Lorna Yes, I remember all that. But you seem not to remember, sir, how perilous a place this is.

John I'm frightened, all the time I don't look at you. I'm sorry if I seem to speak out of turn. I must look a great churl to you. I'll learn to speak softly, and perhaps I might take up a musical instrument.(**Lorna** *laughs, as embarrassed as he is*) Mistress Lorna, I will go. I don't wish to alarm you. If any rogue shot me, it would grieve you. At least I hope it would. And it would break my mother's heart. Few mothers have such a son as me. That is her view, Mistress Lorna, and I speak it modestly. Try to think of me, now and then. I will bring you some eggs. Our little blue hen be just starting.

Lorna Thank you, but you mustn't come. But if you do, you can leave them here for me. But you mustn't come again.

John No. But I will. I'll come three times a day.

He takes her hand in his, then dances away, singing and waving. She runs to him to shush him, laughing, then goes, waving. They both turn, stay looking at each other across the acting space.

The Ridd Household

Mrs. Ridd and Lizzie enter and sit at table.

Mrs. Ridd And he comes home late for his tea and as love-sick as our Annie. Eat, John, I tell him. A full day in the fields, and you've eaten nothing, and he sits gazing at his plate as if he can see a face in it.

Lizzie (*imitating John*) What's that you say?

Mrs. Ridd See! I might as well talk to the hay-rick.

Lizzie Annie goes like this! Every time she sees Tom Faggus she goes dreamy and droopy, just like our John.

Mrs. Ridd I'd like to meet the maid that was good enough for our John.

Lizzie He goes out in his best clothes, and he comes home dripping wet.

Mrs. Ridd He fell in the river, fishing for loach.

Lizzie In his best clothes?

Mrs. Ridd And what does he say to that? Nothing. He ups and goes, and not a bite eaten! Here, eat it up, Lizzie. You're not in love, so you've still got an appetite for good food, thank the lord. (*She and Lizzie exit*)

OLD JOHN And not long after I was there again, risking my neck, with my pockets stuffed with eggs for her. And when I gave them to her, she cried. 'It just comes over me sometimes, when I smell new hay like that', she said. 'I'm not used to such kindness.'

The Doone Valley

Choughs or jackdaws calling. **Lorna** *and* **John** *approach each other. He gives her the eggs.*

OLD JOHN I wanted to put my arms round her, but I was too shy.

JOHN Who looks after you?

LORNA I have no memory of my mother or father. They say my father was the oldest son of Sir Ensor, and they call me heiress to this little realm of violence.

JOHN But who cares for you, like my mother cares for me?

LORNA My grandfather, Sir Ensor. He's always very stern and harsh, except with me. I should be happy, John, because it is a very beautiful place to live in, sheltered from the winter cold and the summer heat. But all around me is violence and robbery, coarseness and savagery. I live under a curse that will last for ever. (*she cries*)

JOHN Please don't cry. Here, rest your head on me, let me wipe your eyes. But please don't cry. I could cry myself at the thought of you living among such harshness, and no-one to care for you.

LORNA I have a little Cornish maid called Gwenny Carfax. She is fond of me, I know. She lives at home with me. But can I call this home? I have read that there are places on earth where people love each other and treat each other with kindness.

JOHN Aye, mistress Lorna, there are such places.

LORNA How I would love to know such happiness myself. John Ridd, you bring me great happiness by coming here, but I fear for you and I fear for myself.

John Then I'll stay away.

Lorna No! I couldn't bear that. But come less often. Come a month today.

John And if you need me before then, how will I know?

Lorna I'll drape this black shawl over the boulder by the stream.

John That's good. I shall watch it every day.

Lorna And you will come a month today?

John The very first Monday of March. I promise thee, dear Lorna Doone.

They touch hands, shyly, and go in opposite directions.

Old John Every day I thought of her, and longed to see her. But at the end of the month I was forced to leave home, and it broke my heart to go. This is what happened.

The Ridd Household

John enters. Old John picks up a broom and hands it to him.

Old John I was sweeping the yard, and whistling, and thinking only of Lorna, when a stranger hailed me.

Stickles Service of the King! Service of our lord the King! Come hither, thou great yokel, at risk of fine and imprisonment.

John What be ye wanting?

Stickles Plover Barrows Farm. God only knows how tired I be. Is there anywhere in this cursed country a cursed place called Plover Barrows farm? For the last twenty miles at least everybody tells me it's only half a mile further, or only just round the corner. If you tell me that too I'd be inclined to thump you, except you be three times my size.

20

John Spare yourself the trouble sir. This is Plover Barrow's farm, and you are very welcome. Sheep's kidneys is for supper, and the ale is bright from the barrel.

Stickles Sheep's kidneys is good, very good, if they do them without burning. But I can't rest, or bite bread, until I have seen John Ridd. God grant that he be not far away, or I must eat my boots.

John Have no fear, good sir. You have seen John Ridd. I am he, and not likely to go hiding under a bush.

Stickles It would take a big bush to hide you, John Ridd. In the name of the King, His Majesty King James, these presents!

*Stickles hands **John** a parchment scroll. **Mrs. Ridd** and **Annie** run on excitedly.*

John It says John Ridd! John Ridd! My name. Look mother, writ large!

Mrs. Ridd John Ridd!

Stickles Read on, son, read on thou great fool, if you can stammer more than your own name. There is nothing there to kill thee, boy, and my supper will be spoiling. Don't stare at me like that, you fool. You're big enough to eat me. Read, read, read.

John If you please, sir, tell me your name, and why you've brought me this.

Stickles Jeremy Stickles is my name, lad, nothing more than a poor servant of the worshipful Court of King's bench. And at this moment a starving one, and no supper for me until you read.

Mrs. Ridd Yes, read it John, or I shall faint away with wondering.

John (*reading*) To our good subject John Ridd, being held in high respect throughout the parish of Oare –

Annie High respect, John!

OLD JOHN It was a summons from King James himself to present myself immediately to the high justice of his court. It gave no reason, save that the matter was urgent.

JOHN When must I go?

STICKLES You read the words. The matter is full urgent, John Ridd. One night's rest for me, and then we must be off.

JOHN Well, I can't go.

MRS. RIDD Can't go, John? A journey to London is dark and dangerous, but you're on King's business, and this good man will be with thee.

JOHN No, it's not that. Not fear. I can't go, and that's it.

STICKLES Can't go, he says? It is an order, John Ridd.

JOHN But Monday is the first of the month. And I am promised ... No, I can't go. No, I can't, mother.

MRS. RIDD Come you in, Master Stickles. Tis the shock. He'll go with you, I'll see to that. For all his size, he's bashful, and not used to having honour bestowed on him. But he will go.

Stickles, Mrs. Ridd and Annie go.

JOHN Oh Lorna, my lovely Lorna, watching and waiting for me. You will be there by the waterfall on Monday next, I know that well. If only I could tell thee. My heart will be with thee, every step of my journey. But what will you think of me, breaking my word like this?

The Doone Valley

Gwenny Carfax is brushing Lorna's hair.

GWENNY He's not worth a tear, Miss Lorna. No man is. I tell thee, they all let you down in the end. Now don't start crying again. I tell you, they're not worth it.

LORNA I'm sure you're right Gwenny. But don't go on so. I won't shed another tear, if you promise not to go on.

Sir Ensor Doone *enters with* ***Counsellor*** *and* ***Carver***.

SIR ENSOR You've kept me waiting, Lorna. I don't like it.

GWENNY She wasn't well, Sir Ensor.

SIR ENSOR Go away Gwenny. I want to talk to her on her own. (***Gwenny*** *leaves, but stays within earshot*) Now Lorna. I'm an old man, not getting any stronger. I want you settled before I go.

LORNA I don't understand.

SIR ENSOR You understand me very well. High time. High time, Lorna.

CARVER For marriage.

COUNSELLOR For marriage.

LORNA Not for many years, grandfather. I'm too young to think of such things.

SIR ENSOR That's as may be, but before I die, the betrothal promise must be made between yourself and Carver.

LORNA To marry Carver? Marriage to Carver Doone! That will never happen.

SIR ENSOR It will Lorna. He is a fine, strong man. When I am gone he will take my place at the head of the Doones. And you will be at his side. Make no mistake about it.

Sir Ensor and Counsellor *leave.* ***Carver*** *places his hand on* ***Lorna's*** *shoulder. She shrinks away from him. He laughs and leaves, whistling his tuneless notes.* ***Gwenny*** *runs in and clasps* ***Lorna*** *in her arms.*

LORNA My life is ended if I have to marry Carver. Please make John come to me. Oh please, please. (*they go*)

OLD JOHN But I knew nothing of this. What criminals these men of law are! There was I, lodging at my own expense for two whole months, calling daily to the King's bench as requested, and being told daily that my case must wait, they were too busy with other matters. And I still had no idea why I had been sent for. At last I was called to the presence of Judge Jeffreys.

Judge Jeffreys' Study

John enters, uncertain what to do, torn between humility and anger. ***Judge Jeffreys*** *is writing at a desk, and doesn't look up.*

JOHN If it please your worship, here I am according to order, awaiting your pleasure.

JEFFREYS John Ridd. So, you have come. We have brought you a long way, and will proceed to question you.

JOHN And I am ready to answer, unless I'm asked things I don't know about, or shouldn't speak of on my honour.

JEFFREYS Thou hadst better answer me everything, lump. What have you to do with honour? Now, is there in your neighbourhood a certain nest of rogues, robbers and outlaws?

JOHN Yes, my lord. I believe some of them to be robbers, and all of them are outlaws.

JEFFREYS And what is your high sheriff about, that he doesn't hang them all? Or send them up to me to hang? Eh?

JOHN I reckon that he is afraid, my lord. It is not safe to meddle with them. Their place is very strong.

JEFFREYS What is the name of this pestilent race, and how many of them are there?

JOHN They are the Doones of Bagworthy Forest, may it please your worship. And we reckon there be about forty of them, beside the women and children.

JEFFREYS Forty Doones, and all of them thieves! And women and children! Thunder of God. How long have they been there?

JOHN Thirty years, my lord. Or forty. They came before the great war, longer back than I can remember.

JEFFREYS Aye, long before you were born, John. Good, you speak plainly. Woe betide a liar if I get hold of him. Now, have you ever seen a man called Tom Faggus?

JOHN Yes sir, many and many a time. He and our Annie–

JEFFREYS Tom Faggus is a good man. Thoroughly straightforward. Pays his fines, like a good man. Nevertheless, John, he will come to the gallows. Tell him this from me. I will never condemn him myself, but others forget his good nature. Tell him to change his name, turn parson, or do anything that will make it wrong to hang him. Parson would be the best thing, he has the right face for it.

JOHN Thank you sir. I'll be sure to tell him that.

JEFFREYS Now, a few more things, and then you can go. Is there any sign of unrest against his majesty King James where you live?

JOHN None at all, sir. We pray for him in church, hoping it may do him good. And we talk about him a little afterwards. But after that nothing else is said.

JEFFREYS That is the way it should be, and the least said the better. But there are things happening elsewhere in Devon – but I see you know nothing of them. It won't be long before all England hears of them, I fear. Now John, I've taken a liking to you, because no man has ever told me the truth without fear of favour more thoroughly and readily than you. Keep clear of that unrest in Devon. Many men will swing high for it. Even I could not save you. *(stern)* And keep away from the Doones, John Ridd.

The Doone Valley

Lorna places the black shawl on the rock.

End of Act One

ACT TWO

The Ridd Household

Backlit tableau of men working in the fields. Sound of curlews or skylarks.

OLD JOHN Two months waiting, and then to be ordered to keep away from Lorna! It took me a further two weeks to walk home from London, but every step I took was lighter with thoughts of seeing her again no matter what Judge Jeffreys said. And it was so good to be coming home, to hear the curlews on the moors again, and to see the hawthorns white with blossom.

Mrs. Ridd and Annie are sewing. Lizzie runs in, followed by John, who is carrying a bundle slung across his back.

LIZZIE It's John. John's come home at last!

MRS. RIDD John! *(hugs him)* Oh, how we've longed for news of you. You've been away so long! Feasting and merrymaking no doubt, with the King himself! What promotion has he given you?

JOHN No promotion, only sore feet.

MRS. RIDD Walking! You could have been killed. Oh, thank God you weren't killed! No, I'm not weeping. I'm not weeping.

ANNIE What did they want you for, if they weren't giving you promotion?

JOHN News of Oare. I would not want to have promotion. I would not want any place but this to live in, and you and my sisters to live with – except…

LIZZIE Except your sweetheart, whoever she may be. What's in that sack?

Annie Lizzie, don't pester him. You can see he's weary to the very bones. Food he wants, and his own bed, and none of your chatter.

Mrs. Ridd Sit at the table, John. I'll warm up the stew. The very best stew it should be, the best in the world, not this mean stuff.

Lizzie I'll take your sack. But it's so heavy! Is it presents? Can I open it?

John I'll do it. (*hands presents out*) A shawl for mother. A brush set for Annie.

Annie A hair brush. And a mirror! How pretty.

Lizzie Pity it doesn't have a pretty picture inside it. But isn't there anything else, John? Who's this little box for?

John Leave it! Don't touch that!

Lizzie Then it's for your lady love. Who is she, John Ridd?

John And a book of poetry for Lizzie.

Lizzie John, John, I have prayed every night of my life for such a thing! You are the best brother ever!

Lizzie and Annie run out with their presents. Mrs. Ridd sits by John, holding his hands.

Mrs. Ridd I don't mind about your promotion. I don't care two figs about it. I am just glad to have you safe home. But why did His Majesty send for you?

John I didn't actually speak to His Majesty. It was Judge Jeffreys I spoke to, and he's a strange, fearsome, kind man who questioned me very severely. He wanted to know about the Doones.

Mrs. Ridd The Doones! But they're nothing to do with us, nor ever will be, thank God.

John No. So I told him.

Mrs. Ridd There's such a sadness about you, my son. Can you share it with me?

John I wish I could. No, it's not sadness. Weariness.

Mrs. Ridd Tomorrow is Sunday. Spend the whole day resting. (*they go*)

Old John But I had no thoughts of resting! Lorna, that was all that was on my mind. I must see Lorna and make my peace with her. I set off with the dawn, and half way up the hillside I spied her black shawl on the rock. My heart was in my mouth with dread. I ran the rest of the way.

The Doone Valley

*Lorna picks her shawl from the boulder. **John** enters, breathless.*

John Lorna!

Lorna turns and stares at him, not moving.

John Mistress Lorna. I saw the shawl on the rock. I thought you were in need of me.

Lorna Oh yes sir. Indeed I was. But that was weeks ago.

Old John Oh how heavy my heart was! I wanted to explain, but she was so cold to me. I nearly went back home, but I saw sorrow in her face.

John puts his arms round her.

John My darling Lorna. Do you love me?

Lorna I like you very much.

John But do you love me? Do you love me more than all the world?

Lorna No, of course not! Why should I?

John I don't know. I just hoped you did.

Lorna I like you very much, Master Ridd, and I think about you nearly every day.

John That's not enough. I think about you every instant of my life. I would give up my home for you, I would give up everything in the world for you. My family, my life, my hope of life beyond it. Don't you love me as much as this?

Lorna No, I don't. Don't talk so wild. If you like me so much, why do you leave me for people like Carver to marry me?

John (*broken*) Carver? You have married Carver?

Lorna No John, not yet. But they want me to marry him, and he's twice my age!

John takes a jewel box out of his pocket.

John See what I have for thee, from London town. Sapphires to match your blue veins, and pearls to match your white fingers. *(he puts a ring on her finger)*

Lorna Oh, you crafty Master Ridd! I thought you were much too simple ever to do this kind of thing. No wonder you're so good at catching fish.

John And have I caught you, my little fish? Or must all my life be spent in hopeless angling for you?

Lorna (*takes off the ring, kisses it, and returns it to him*) I daren't take it now. It would not be fair to you, because I can make no promises. I will try to love you as much as you deserve and wish.

Keep it for me until then. I will earn it back, I know I will. Perhaps you will be sorry, when it's all too late, to be loved by someone like me.

John I would die happily if you just told me once that you loved me.

Lorna You must go. And you must stay away. They watch me all the time.

John When can I come back to you?

Lorna In two months. One for your safety, one for mine. It must be so. Promise me you won't come back before then. Please go. Don't squeeze me so hard, you don't know your own strength. Two months, and I'll tell you.

Laughing, she pushes him away, then runs off. **John** *watches her, then goes in the other direction.*

Old John So. I had a secret, a precious secret hope burning in my heart. One day Lorna would marry me! But when I came home, Annie told me something that I would rather not know – that she intended to marry that highwayman, Tom Faggus. My poor foolish sister! And in return for her secret she took mine.

Annie (*enters to audience*) He wants to marry Lorna Doone! I fear she has made a fool of him. I watch him toil up that hill to see her night after night after his work is done, and I see him come home sad and worried. Lorna is never there. (*goes*)

Old John But I thought no-one else knew about Lorna. Then one day our milkmaid Betty Muxworthy came looking for me, crafty with knowledge.

The Ridd Household

John pensive. ***Betty Muxworthy*** *creeps up on him.*

Betty Larna Doone.

John What was that, Betty?

Betty Oi zed Larna Doone. You heard. You bin going up there, night after night.

John Keep your voice down.

Betty Night after night, Oi've seed thee. And she bain't there for you, be she?

John If you know something, tell me.

Betty Gwenny Carfax bin down here, looking for thee.

John What's happened? For God's sake, Betty.

Betty Give me a message for thee, secret loike.

John Well? Tell me!

Betty Goo of a morning, thee girt soft. Her can't get out of an evening now, her hath zent word to me to tell thee.

John Betty, you're wonderful!

He flings his arms round her and kisses her. Runs off.

Betty Oh, fie on thee Jan Ridd! Lunnon impudence Oi call that. Do it again!

The Doone Valley

Birdsong.

Old John The wild orchids were out by the river, it was summer again, and my Lorna was waiting for me. And she had the answer to my questions. Yes, she loved me. Yes, she would give her life to me.

John and *Lorna* enter, their arms round each other. *John* puts the ring on her finger.

LORNA But who am I, to even dream of it? Something in my heart tells me that it can never, never be.

JOHN Now you must think what it means, Lorna. You will be a lowly yeoman's wife.

LORNA What more could I wish for? But after all the crime and outrage wrought by my family, I can't believe I will ever know the peace and comfort of an ordinary household. With all my heart I long for such a home.

JOHN And with all my heart I long for you to have one, and to share it forever with me. *(he embraces her and they go)*

OLD JOHN I ran home with my heart soaring. Soon I would be bringing Lorna home with me. Now at last I could tell my mother about her. But I found her and Annie in a state of tears.

The Ridd Household

Mrs. Ridd and *Annie* are both crying. *Lizzie* reads, unperturbed.

MRS. RIDD John – is that John? Come over here and talk sense to your ridiculous sister. Oh, how she has vexed me today! She wants to marry Tom Faggus the highwayman!

John approaches and sits down, taking her hand.

JOHN Since you know Annie's secret, you must know mine too. I love somebody. And today she promised to be my wife.

Mrs. Ridd That's no surprise. But pray God you have made a more sensible match than Annie has.

John I have, though you may not see it that way. I am in love with Lorna Doone.

Lizzie (*laughs*) Lorna Doone!

Mrs. Ridd Lorna Doone! A child of murderers and thieves! Keep away from her. Keep away. Tell me it's just a cruel joke, and there's no truth in it. Oh, to have two such foolish children as you and Annie. A better mother never lived, so you keep saying to me, and I believed you. What kind of a mother is it who brings her children to this?

John When you meet her, you will love her too. She is very young, and very beautiful, and very tender hearted, and loves you even before she has met you.

Mrs. Ridd Well. So be it. Bring her to meet me. There are some very good sausages left over, am I right, Annie?

John As if Lorna would eat sausages! Lorna eating sausages!

Mrs. Ridd And why not? If she means to be a farmer's wife she must take to farmers' ways. What do you think, Annie?

Annie She will eat them if John asks her to, particularly as I made them.

John If only I could try! You only need to see her once, and you'd never want her to go away. And she would love you with all her heart, she's so good and gentle.

Mrs. Ridd Well, that's lucky. Otherwise she'd soon turn me out of the farm, as she has you so completely under her thumb. I see that my time is over. Lizzie and I will have to seek our fortunes out there.

John Will you have the kindness to stop talking nonsense? Everything belongs to you, and that includes your children. And you belong to us. Why do you make Annie cry like this? You ought to know better.

Mrs. Ridd I want the best for you both. I'm an old fool, that's why.

Annie Not an *old* fool mother. You only have one grey hair in your head and – *(she pulls it out)* there! It's gone!

Lights dim. Howling wind.

Lizzie *(to audience)* So, it looks as if my foolish brother and sister will be having their way. But we have a farm to run, and have to get on with it. Autumn's over, all the apples are down in the gales, and there's a cold wind that's howling for snow. And a visitor comes to the door.

Stickles *(outside)* Service of the King!

Lizzie It's him again! Service of the King! Eat all our good chops, that's the only service he wants.

John Come in Master Stickles, and welcome.

Stickles *(enters)* Good day to you ma'am, Mistress Annie, Mistress Lizzie. I'm on the King's business, and will eat with you tonight.

Mrs. Ridd And welcome.

Stickles I'll be staying some time, Mistress Ridd.

Mrs. Ridd We're very honoured. I'll get a room ready. *(she and **Annie** go)*

Stickles I need a man to stable my horse, and groom him, and have him ready day or night whenever I need it.

Lizzie Are they fire-arms, Master Stickles?

Stickles They are indeed, and loaded, and they stay in my room with me, and my sharp sword besides. Ready at all times. Take my boots off, Mistress Lizzie. They have mud on the soles and lord only knows what else, from the farmyard. Take them and clean them for me.

LIZZIE Does the king say so?

STICKLES He does. All is in service of His Majesty the King.

Lizzie carries the boots outside, giggling.

JOHN Are there more of you, might I ask?

STICKLES I must swear you to the utmost secrecy.

JOHN I can hold my tongue.

STICKLES I have many men at my disposal, but they are all stationed elsewhere.

JOHN Thank God for that. This little house will be turned upside down as it is.

STICKLES You have some right to know the meaning of all this, being trusted as you were by the Lord Chief Justice. But he found you a bit leisurely. Not too quick in the head.

JOHN I'm sure you're right. What job is it?

STICKLES In ten words, so as not to tax your poor brains too much, I am here to watch the hatching of a secret plot. Ssh! Tell no-one. Now listen to me, because I wish you well. Stick to the winning side, and have nothing to do with the other one.

JOHN That's exactly what I intend to do, if I only knew which was the winning side. (*they go*)

Bitterly cold wind. **Annie** *enters with logs.*

ANNIE (*to audience*) Master Stickles shows no sign of leaving us. He'll be here till Christmas at this rate, and he's been demanding a fire in his room day and night, and I've had to chop all the logs. But why is he here? King's business, that's all I know. (*goes*)

OLD JOHN And I was worried by what Master Stickles had told me, remembering what Judge Jeffreys had told me, too. I was very frightened that the Doones were involved and my Lorna was affected by it. I kept going up there, but she was never where we usually met. I even searched for her in Carver Doone's cottage, and a rough, loathsome place it was, I tell you. But Lorna was nowhere. It seemed as if she was dead, and that bleak wind was her funeral hymn. I had to find out.

The Doone Valley

Night. **Ridley** *and* **other man** *are playing cards by lantern light.* **John** *enters cautiously, hoots, and their lantern goes out.*

OLD JOHN There was a light in a lower window of Sir Ensor Doone's house. I made straight for it, praying that Lorna was there!

JOHN (*whispers under* **Sir Ensor's** *window*) Lorna! Lorna!

RIDLEY Who's there? Answer, or I fire at thee. (**John** *whistles* **Carver's** *tuneless notes*) Master Carver! I did not see thee in the dark. I'll leave thee private. (*goes*)

JOHN Lorna! Open the window. It's me. (**Lorna** *opens the window*) Lorna! Don't you know me?

LORNA John! Oh, you must be mad!

JOHN As mad as a march hare without any news of my darling. You knew I'd come. Why are you locked up here?

LORNA My poor grandfather is very ill. I'm afraid he's dying. The Counsellor and Carver are masters of the valley now. I tried to send a signal for you but Carver caught me. And little Gwenny isn't allowed to leave the valley.

GWENNY (*out of sight*) Miztrezz Lorna, what be ye doing with the window wide open?

Lorna Gwenny, it's you! Come and meet John.

Gwenny Jan Ridd? Here? Whoy! The size of that man! Thee be a giant!

John I'm pleased to meet you at last, little maid.

Gwenny Whoy, a giant and a gentleman! I shall know thee again, young man, no fear of that. Now missis, goo on courtin', and I'll gae ootside and keep watch. (*she goes*)

Lorna She's the best little thing in the world. Now, no more of your 'courtin', John Ridd! I love you too much, truly, truly. You must go. Go, if you love me, go.

John I can feel you trembling. How can I leave you like this?

Lorna You'll make me cry if you go on like this. You know we can never be together. Everyone is against it. Try not to think about me any more.

John And will you stop thinking about me?

Lorna Of course I will, if you agree to it. At least I'll try.

John I'll find a way to save you from all this. Trust me. (*he goes*)

The Ridd Household

Stickles (*to audience*) I have too much work here. I'm heartily sorry I accepted this commission – to extract taxes from the smugglers on these coasts, to keep an eye on the Doones, and to sniff out any plots against the Crown. Too much for one man. Matters grow worse, not better. The only thing I can do with any chance of success is to rout out these vile Doone fellows. Burn the roofs over their heads.

Old John Destroy the town of the Doones! I was worried sick at the idea. And all the Doones inside it! Surely he would never think of such a cruel act as that!

Stickles (*to audience*) A cruel act! It would be a mercy for at least three counties. No-one is crueller than the Doones.

Tableau of opening scene, with child's scream.

Old John I told him I would have nothing to do with it. I would not strike a blow against the Doone village.

John *enters stage between Ridd Household and Doone Valley.*

Stickles They are your father's murderers, John. You owe his revenge.

John *goes towards* **Doone Valley. Gwenny** *is watching for him.*

Gwenny Young man, you must come with me. Old man be dying, and he won't go until he has words with thee.

John What can he want with me? Has Lorna told him?

Gwenny She has, zeeing 'em coming to such a low ebb. But he was so vexed about thy low blood that he all but come to life again to beat thee!

She leads him to **Sir Ensor** *in bed,* **Lorna** *holding his hand.* **Gwenny** *goes.*

Sir Ensor (*weak*) Ah! Are you that great John Ridd?

John John Ridd is my name, your honour, and I hope your worship is better.

Sir Ensor Child, have you sense enough to know what you have been doing?

John I have set my eyes far above my rank.

Sir Ensor Are you ignorant of the fact that Lorna Doone is born of one the oldest families in Europe?

John Sir, the Ridds of Oare have been honest men twice as long as the Doones have been rogues.

Sir Ensor Listen to me boy, or clown, or fool, or whatever you are. Listen to the words of an old man who has not many hours to live. There is nothing in this world to fear, nothing to trust, nothing to hope for, and nothing, nothing to love.

John I hope your worship is not quite right.

Sir Ensor Thus I forbid you ever to see this foolish child again. You will pledge your word in Lorna's presence never to see her or seek her again, never even to think of her. Get it done, for I'm weary. (**Lorna** *rises and goes to* **John**. *They look at each other with great love, brave, saying nothing*) Ye two fools. Ye two fools.

John May it please your worship, maybe we are not such fools as we look. But if we are, we are happy, so long as we may be two fools together.

Sir Ensor Why, John, you are not altogether the clumsy yokel and clod that I took you for. I know little of the world, but this is beyond all I've seen. (*very weak now, takes a necklace from under his pillow*) Here child, take this necklace. It's yours. Fools you are. Be fools for ever. It is the best thing I can wish for you. Boy and girl, be boy and girl, until you have grandchildren. (*sinks back on his pillow*)

Lorna (*sobs*) Uncle!

Lights down. Cold wind. **Old John** *enters with lantern. Suggestion of snow.*

Old John After Sir Ensor died they locked my Lorna up. They starved her and Gwenny so she would agree to marry Carver. By the time I found her again she could barely speak for weakness. I knew I would not be leaving the Doone Valley again without her. If they killed me, we would die together. Snow was piled high around our house, the rivers were frozen solid. I brought a sledge and a sealskin coat, and when I lifted her up she was like a child in my arms.

The Ridd Household

Warm fire flickering. **John** *carries* **Lorna** *in and lays her on the couch in front of the fire.* **Lizzie** *and* **Annie** *gather round her.* **Gwenny** *stands in the doorway.* **Mrs. Ridd** *enters.*

John Mother, here she is. Here's your daughter. I've brought her home.

End of Act Two

ACT THREE

The Ridd Household

Spring.

OLD JOHN So, Lorna entered our household, and went straight to my mother's heart by the road of pity, smoothed by grace, and youth, and gentleness. And she was just as readily loved as a sister by Annie and Lizzie.

Mrs. Ridd, Lizzie, John and Lorna are dining. Lorna wears her necklace.

MRS. RIDD What a princess you look, Lorna, with that lovely necklace on.

LORNA Thank you. It's precious to me because my grandfather gave it to me, but apart from that, it's worthless.

Annie enters with Tom Faggus. He kisses Lorna's hand.

ANNIE (*to audience*) But that's not what my dear Tom thinks. Tom Faggus, ex-highwayman, pardoned by the king for all his past crimes, my husband! – can't take his eyes off Lorna! (*laughs fondly and goes with Lizzie and Lorna*)

FAGGUS What do you know of the history of that beautiful maiden, good mother?

MRS. RIDD Not half so much as my son. And when John chooses not to tell a thing, wild horses won't drag it out of him.

FAGGUS You understand each other well. Ah, if only I'd had a mother, how different I might have been! I have seen your beautiful young lady before, John. Many years ago, when she was a little child. I can't remember any more about it, but I remember her eyes.

John Have you ever been in the Doone Valley?

Faggus Never. I value my life too much for that. You know, you are putting your home and yourselves at great risk by keeping her here. Is she worth it, in spite of her great beauty?

John I'll ask your opinion when I want it.

Faggus Bravo, our John Ridd! Fools will be fools till the end of the world. I'd be the same. But don't let that helpless child go round with a thing worth half the county on her.

John She's worth all the county, and all England too. But the ring I gave her cost no more than I could afford.

Faggus Tush! I'm not talking about the ring! The necklace, you great oaf! The necklace is worth all your farm, and your Uncle Reuben's fortune, aye, much more still.

John It's made of glass. Ask her. *(calls)* Lorna.

Faggus Glass indeed! They're the finest brilliants I've ever set eyes on, and I've handled a good many in my chequered past.

Mrs. Ridd Glory!

Lorna comes in.

Mrs. Ridd Lorna dear, may Tom look at your necklace?

Lorna Of course. I had it when I was a little girl, and my grandfather looked after it for me. But it's only a trinket.

Faggus *(holding it up)* Do you think it is worth five pounds?

Lorna It's very bright and very pretty, but I'm sure it can't be worth that much.

Faggus What a chance for a bargain! If it weren't for my promise to Annie I could make my fortune!

LORNA Sir, I wouldn't sell it you for twenty times that much. I think it belonged to my mother.

FAGGUS There are twenty five rose diamonds in it and twenty five large brilliants that can't be matched in London.

MRS. RIDD Lord save us!

FAGGUS How say you to a hundred thousand pounds?

LORNA Dear mother, I'm so glad! I want you to have it. It would make me so happy.

MRS. RIDD Indeed no! Indeed I could never accept such a gift.

FAGGUS Whatever you do with it, Mistress Lorna, don't wear it. Promise me that. It is very old, and very rare, and priceless. Guard it with your life. (*they go, or lights down*)

OLD JOHN But by nightfall we had far more to worry about than Lorna's necklace. Our farm was attacked by the Doones themselves, led by Carver.

Carver and others run on, with lanterns and brandishing pistols. Sounds (offstage) of horses neighing. **John, Tom, Stickles** *and others run on.*

OLD JOHN They let loose all our horses. We ran out, Tom Faggus, Jeremy Stickles, farm boys, with all the tools and weapons we could lay our hands on. Then I heard Carver shout.

CARVER Two of you dolts go and make us a light to cut the Ridd's throats by. There are two other damsels here; you may take them away if you want. And the mother. She's still comely. Kill every man and child and burn the cursed place down. But one thing. If any man touches Lorna I will stab him where he stands. She belongs to me.

Men shout and run off, followed and tackled by **Ridd men**. *Mimed fighting.* **Two Doones** *die.* **John** *aims his gun at* **Carver**.

John (*to audience*) I set my gun against his breast, I see the sight of brass glimmering on either side. The aim is as sure as death itself. If I draw the trigger, Carver Doone will breathe no more. Yet I cannot pull the trigger. For I have never taken human life, nor done bodily harm to any man. (*to **Carver***) Do you call yourself a man?

Carver Who's there?

John (*knocks **Carver's** gun out of his hand*) Carver Doone, you are a despicable villain. I may not be your match in craft, but I am in manhood. Lie in your native muck.

*Slowly **John** brings **Carver** down with great strength. Lights down.*

The Ridd Household

*Daylight. Enter **Counsellor Doone**.*

Counsellor (*to audience*) Counsellor Doone, oozing charm, prepares to spellbind these simple Ridds.

***Mrs. Ridd** enters with **Lorna**.*

Counsellor And pretends he has come to see how his precious little niece is faring. (*kisses **Mrs. Ridd's** hand*) Your company is charming, Mistress Ridd.

Mrs. Ridd So kind, your honour.

Counsellor (*to Lorna*) My darling child, my dearest niece, how wonderfully well you look. Mistress Ridd, I give you credit. I would never have believed our Queen could look so royal. Dearest Lorna, kiss your uncle.

Lorna I'm sorry sir, but you've smoked tobacco.

Counsellor The dear child! Her grandfather was noted for his olfactory powers too. I come about your son. I can hardly be wrong in assuming that this armigure must be the too attractive cynosure to our poor little maiden. Are you with me Mrs. Ridd? I'll come to the point. Mistress Ridd, as Lorna's guardian, are you following? I give full and ready consent to her marriage to your son.

Mrs. Ridd Oh, how good you are! How kind! Well, I always did say that the most learned men were the best and kindest.

Counsellor Quite so. What a goodly couple they'll be. And if we can add him to our strength –

Mrs. Ridd Oh no sir! No! You mustn't think of it. He has always been brought up so honest.

Counsellor Hmm. That makes a difference. Honesty is a decided disqualification for life among the Doones. But surely he might get over these prejudices?

Mrs. Ridd Never. He couldn't. He never can. When he was only that high, sir, he couldn't even steal an apple.

Counsellor Ah, then I fear his case is incurable. A man like him is no use at all. And Lorna, it is high time you knew the truth of the whole matter. Your father slew dear John's father, and dear John's father slew yours.

Mrs. Ridd You old villain! What is the good of quality, if this is what comes of it? You know the words that make mischief, but not the words that heal them. Out of my way! (*she goes with* **Lorna**)

Annie *enters with pail.*

Counsellor (*to audience*) The fair sex can be very touchy. You might as well put a wild bird in a cage as expect a woman to be reasonable. Now, I didn't find what I'm looking for. But never mind. I will have it.

ANNIE (*to audience*) And having failed to charm my mother, he turns his attention to me. He finds me in the dairy, making cream.

COUNSELLOR Have you heard that if you pass a string of beads across the top, the cream will set three times as solid, and in thrice the quantity?

ANNIE No sir, I never heard of that. What a thing it is to read books, and to grow learned! But we can try it with my coral necklace. It won't be witch-craft will it?

COUNSELLOR Certainly not. I'll do it myself. But coral will not do child, neither will anything coloured. The beads must be of plain common glass, but the brighter they are, the better.

ANNIE Then I know the very thing. Lorna has a necklace of some old glass beads. Bright as bright, they be.

COUNSELLOR My dear, they cannot be as bright as your own pretty eyes. But remember one thing, Annie. You must not say what it is for, or even that I'm going to use it, or anything at all about it, or the charm will be broken.

ANNIE (*to audience*) And off I run to fetch Lorna's necklace, thinking what a kind man he is, and not at all the way I expected a Doone to be. (*she goes*)

COUNSELLOR What sweet fools these country maidens are.

Annie enters with necklace.

ANNIE Here it is sir! Look how it sparkles.

COUNSELLOR Oh, that old thing. I remember that old thing well enough. I suppose it will do. Three times three I pass it over. Crinkleum, crankum, grass and clover! What are you afraid of, you silly child?

ANNIE Good sir, it is perfect witchcraft! I'm sure of that, because it rhymes! What would mother say to me? Shall I ever go to heaven now? Oh, I can see the cream already!

Counsellor Now, not a word of this to a living soul. You mustn't come back in here for three hours at least. By that time the charm will have done its work. The pan will be cream right to the bottom, and you will bless me for a secret that has made your fortune. Put the bauble under this lid; no-one must lift it for a day and a night. Have no fear, my simple wench; not a breath of harm shall come to you if you obey my orders.

Annie Oh that I will, sir, that I will.

Counsellor Now go to your room without a single word to anyone. Bolt yourself in, and three hours from now, read the Lord's prayer backwards.

*As **Annie** runs out, **Counsellor** smiles knowingly at audience, puts necklace in his pocket, and goes. Enter **Mrs. Ridd, Lorna, Annie, Lizzie.***

All Four The necklace – has gone!

*Enter **John** and **Jeremy Stickles**.*

John He has stolen a hundred thousand pounds. Fifty farms like ours cannot make it good to Lorna.

*Exit, **Lorna** comforting **Annie**, **Lizzie** comforting **Mrs. Ridd**.*

Stickles My son, this is very bad news. It cuts me to the heart to hear of such a deadly blow to you and your mother, and this farm. How long has it been in the family?

John For about six hundred years. Surely no-one will turn us out? But it is that other matter that grieves me more. Only think of loving Lorna and knowing that her father killed mine.

Stickles Then think how Lorna feels. If I can ease you of this burden, are you strong enough to bear another?

John Say what you have to say.

STICKLES Sit down John. I'll tell you a story. Imagine this is an inn-room in Watchett.

JOHN Watchett! I remember that from my boyhood. But what does it have to do with me now?

Tableau from opening scene. Lights low.

STICKLES Listen. I rested at the inn last night. It was run by a charming Italian woman. And I asked her how she came to be there.

Flashback: An Inn

Candlelit. **Benita** *brings a plate of food to* **Stickles.**

BENITA Buon appetito.

STICKLES What brings a fine Italian lady to Somerset?

BENITA It is a melancholy story, sir.

STICKLES I have a good ear for sad stories, Madam.

BENITA I was travelling from Italy with a very noble English family, an ancient royal family. The young man was killed, and left a wife and baby and a beautiful little girl.

STICKLES That is great tragedy.

BENITA That is not the end of it. My lady asked me to accompany her to England. We arrived by night, and travelled to Watchett, where my lady had a summer castle. But when we arrived our coach was set upon by a troop of horsemen. My lady cried that they were the ancient enemies of her husband's family. I snatched at the most valuable of the jewels, a diamond necklace, and put it on the little girl, hiding it under her cloak.

Stickles A necklace, you say?

Benita The coach was overturned and we were all flung out. I was knocked out by a blow on the head, see, I have the scar to this day. And when I came to, there was my mistress, holding her baby boy in her arms. He was dead, sir, and before morning she had joined him. The attackers took everything, including the beautiful little girl. (*goes*)

End of Flashback

John Who were these people?

Stickles I am as certain as I can be that the robbers were the Doones.

John But what happened to the little girl?

Stickles You great oaf. You are more likely to know than anyone else in the country.

John If I knew I wouldn't be asking. Jeremy, do try to be neither conceited nor thick-headed.

Stickles No-one could be as conceited or thick-headed as you are. As sure as I stand here, that little girl is Lorna. I have brought the maid. Join my soldiers, John. Surely you have more reason than any to take them on. (*goes*)

Lorna enters.

Lorna John, you are full of sad mystery.

John So much to tell you, I hardly know where to start. It all concerns you.

Lorna Nothing else can move me, unless it is about my mother.

John It is. Lorna my darling, you are of an ill-starred race.

Lorna Better than a wicked race. Tell me I'm not a Doone and I will love you even more.

John Here is someone who can tell you just that.

Benita enters.

Benita Mistress Lorna. Mia bella. Do you know me?

Lorna I know your voice. *(overcome)* Is it Benita? Oh, Benita!

They hug each other.

Benita My dear Mistress Lorna, I promise you, you are not one of the Doones.

Lorna But my father – and John's father–

Benita They never even met. Your father was killed in the Pyrenees. Your mother and brother were killed by the Doones.

Lorna Stop. This is more than I can bear.

Benita They snatched you out of my arms and took you away. My darling Lorna, you are not one of them! You are related to His Majesty the King of England!

John goes, shocked by this news. Lorna dazed, watches him go. Enter Commissioner, summoned by Benita.

Commissioner I am told that I will find a person here who goes by the name of Lorna Doone.

Lorna Indeed, you have found her, sir.

Commissioner *(bows)* Lady Lorna Dugal. I come to speak to you in the name of His Majesty the King.

Lights down.

The Ridd Household

Lizzie and *Mrs. Ridd* sewing.

Lizzie Where's Lorna? Ladies are supposed to be good at this sort of thing.

Mrs. Ridd In her room with Gwenny. She has taken all this news very badly, I'm afraid. She's not spoken a word to any of us since, least of all to John.

Lizzie Fancy her being descended from a royal family. The Lady Lorna Dugal!

Mrs. Ridd No, that's not a surprise to me. First time I caught sight of her I thought, why she has more natural dignity about her than anyone I have ever met. And look how she rose above the Doones, with all their coarseness. The only thing they ever got right was to call her their Queen.

Commissioner (*enters*) Good day Mistress. I am returned to escort Lady Dugal now to His Majesty.

Mrs. Ridd I don't understand.

Commissioner My Lady is called to His Majesty's court of Chancery this very day, where she will be under the protection of the Crown until her 21st birthday. Her noble uncle meets us at Dunster. These are my orders.

Lorna enters in rich clothes. **Gwenny** *follows, flustered.*

Mrs. Ridd Lorna, is it true? You're to leave us?

Gwenny She won't say nothing, I tell 'ee. She bin on her knees all mornin', prayin' and cryin'. Don't want titles, nor land, nor money, she says. Only wants her John.

Commissioner Come child, I'm glad to see you ready and prepared.

Mrs. Ridd But you can't take her away like this! Not even a goodbye to John. He wouldn't let you take her if he was here, I promise you that.

Commissioner Madam, save your words. On the orders of His Majesty, she must come, and come now.

Mrs. Ridd (*embraces* **Lorna**) My dear, darling child. (**Lorna**, *upset, says nothing, but follows the* **Commissioner** *out*)

Gwenny She daresn't speak, for fear her heart will break. This letter is for her John. (*goes*)

Sound (offstage) of carriage departing. **Mrs. Ridd** *outside, watching.*

Lizzie (*holds* **Lorna's** *letter to lamp, trying to read it*) My own love – That's easy to say when you're leaving for the Royal Family, that is.

John *enters, and she hides the letter.*

John I thought I heard a carriage at the gate.

Lizzie You should have been here minutes ago. You would have seen it leave this house. (**Mrs. Ridd** *enters*) He heard the carriage.

John Why are looking at me like this? Where's Lorna?

Lizzie Gone.

Mrs. Ridd Whether you will ever see her again depends on her nature, John.

John What do you mean? Have you quarrelled? Why doesn't she come to me? Tell me!

Lizzie The Lady Lorna Dugal is gone to London, brother John, and not likely to come back again. We must try to get on without her.

John My Lorna gone! My Lorna gone! What have you done to her, to make her go away?

Lizzie She is far too grand to be upset by the likes of me. The Lady Lorna Dugal is gone because His Majesty asked for her. How grand she looked too, in the clothes that came for her.

Mrs. Ridd She said not a word to anyone. And she wept enough to break ten hearts. Lizzie has a letter for you, John.

John (*takes letter, reading*) 'My own love. I am almost certain that you would not have let your Lorna go to people who can never, never care for her ...' Dear God. It's true. My darling has gone.

Lights down.

Old John My Lorna had gone, and there was never another word from her. Why didn't she write to me, or send word for me to come for her? Months passed. I toiled in the fields from dawn till dusk, trying to drive her out of my mind. Our men were off fighting, some for the King, some against him. Tom Faggus was with the rebels, which broke Annie's heart. At least the Doones left us quiet. But all I wanted was news of Lorna. Was she well? For Annie's sake I went searching for her Tom, and was arrested for a rebel myself.

Stickles So he is put in my care, and I take him to London and put him in lodgings awaiting a pardon. But I have news for him. I know where he can catch a glimpse of his Lady Lorna. In the King's chapel.

The King's Chapel

*Royal music. Candles. Choir. A **priest** swinging a thurible of incense. A procession of **courtiers**, led by **King** and **Queen**. **Lorna** is with them. She sees **John**, their eyes meet, and she falters and walks on. **John** turns away. **Procession** goes. **Stickles** enters.*

John I can't stay on. I've seen her, and that's enough. She does not want to know me, Jeremy.

Stickles What say you to a little reading matter to lighten your misery?

John I have no heart for reading.

Stickles What say you if it is a letter?

John News from home will only increase my wretchedness. I'll read it later.

Stickles What say you to a letter with the King's seal? And the name, Lady Lorna Dugal?

He holds out the letter. **John** *takes it eagerly.*

John From my darling Lorna. Jeremy, (*hugs him*) you are my dear, dear friend.

The Uncle's House

Gwenny and Lorna are looking out of windows at opposite sides of space.

Lorna Dear Master Ridd. Please come to see me here at my uncle's house. (*sighs*)

Old John Nothing more, after all those cruel months of silence! Yet I went. How could I have stayed away.

Gwenny And here he comes, Girt John Ridd striding to my Lady's house as if he was striding over Exmoor itself.

She opens door to his knock.

John (*enters*) Little Gwenny Carfax! (*he tries to kiss her and she bobs away*)

Gwenny And he needn't expect no welcoming hug from me! Wait here. I'll ask my Lady if she wants to see thee. (*goes*)

John looks round grand room. **Lorna** *enters and waits. He kisses her hand.*

Lorna Is that all?

He embraces her. She cries in his arms.

John Darling Lorna. Darling Lady Lorna. I love you!

Lorna Then why did you behave like that?

John I am behaving. Oh my darling. My only darling!

Lorna Master John Ridd, now I want the truth, the whole truth, and nothing but the truth. Why have you never, for more than a whole year, taken the smallest notice of your old friend, Mistress Lorna Doone?

John For the simple reason that my old friend took no notice of me. I had no idea where to find her.

Lorna What! But all my letters!

John In truth, Lorna, there has never been a letter from you since the day you left.

Lorna But I wrote many times. Many, many! Oh, my poor dear John. But I know who is responsible for this. *(rings bell)* I have often suspected it, but she looks me straight in the face and denies it. (**Gwenny** *enters*) Gwenny, go and fetch the letters which I gave you to send to Mistress Ridd.

Gwenny How can I fetch them when they're gone! It be no use for him to tell no lies.

John Gwenny, will you look at me?

Gwenny I don't want to look at 'ee.

Lorna Now, if you thought it honest to keep the letters, was it honest to keep the money I asked you to send?

Gwenny Oi put the money aside for thee.

Lorna Gwenny, I shall have to send you to the great Justice Jeffreys.

Gwenny Do so. I have done no more than duty and told a heap of lies for your sake. And little gratitude I gets.

Lorna And much gratitude you have shown to someone who did so much for you. Who was that? Answer me.

Gwenny Girt Jan Ridd.

John Why do you treat me like this, Gwenny?

Gwenny Because you be below her so. Her shanna have a poor farming chap. All her land, and all her birth – and who be you, oi'd loike to know?

Lorna Gwenny, you may go. And remember not to come near me for three days. (**Gwenny** *goes, sobbing*) Now she will not eat till she sees me again. But it's the only way to punish her. Make up your mind to one thing, John. If you mean to take me, for better or for worse, you must take Gwenny too.

John I would take you with fifty Gwennies, even though they all hated me. But I don't believe she does, in the bottom of her heart. Yet there is truth in what she says. You are a great lady now.

Lorna John Ridd, listen to me. In the first place, it is quite obvious that neither of us could be happy without the other. And what stands between us? Worldly position, nothing else. I have no more education than you have – less. My blood and ancestry are not a whit purer than yours. We are promised to each other, and we will marry each other. There must be a way. We must ask my uncle to speak to the King for us. But I warn you, he's as deaf as a table. (*they go*)

Old John And her old uncle nodded and smiled and said yes to everything. But I still had to get the King's blessing to marry Lorna, and how was I to get that?

The Ridd Household

Mrs. Ridd There'll be a way, I'm sure of it. Just keep away from those troubles, that's what I tell him.

John Fry staggers in, breathless.

Fry Girt Master Ridd, girt Master Ridd. Where be him? We need him. A terrible deed is done.

Mrs. Ridd Calm yourself, John Fry, calm yourself. Oh, nothing can be as bad as you seem to think it is, nothing.

Fry Oh tes, tes. Nothing in the world be zo bad. Tes them Doones. Twenty sheep gone, oxen, candles, zoider, flour, deer, all in a night. Here there and everywhere they come as they please and takes what they want.

Mrs. Ridd There's nothing new to that, though my heart goes out to their victims. At least they spared us while John was away.

Fry 'Tes all in our neighbourhood. 'Tis as good as on this farm, I tell 'ee. And two maidens lifted from nearby just last night. And Mistress Marjory – One of the finest hen-wives in the county – last night she was feeding her baby and six or seven girt Doones bust in on her, and dragged her off on their horses – And worse, her baby kicked around like a football till it was dead.

Mrs. Ridd Oh, wicked men! Wicked, wicked men. I have never heard of such evil, even from the Doones.

John enters.

Fry All the men are asking for thee. Lead us in, and we'll kill the Doones, every man of them. What do you say, Jan Ridd?

John I'm not a man for violence. You know that.

Fry Jan Ridd, you know the land! Lead us in, lead us in, and we'll take courage from thee, man, and finish them off for ever.

Mrs. Ridd John, this is dangerous.

Fry Tis dangerous to lose, Mistress Ridd, but not to win. What do you say, Jan? We need thee, we need thee.

John Well. I'll come.

*They go towards Doone Valley, joined by **other men**, all carrying torches. Drum beats.*

Men (*chant softly*) For the plundering of our farms, the slaughter of our beasts, we will not forgive thee, Doones.

Women (*watching from Ridd household*) For the rape of our women, for the murder of our children, we will not forgive thee, Doones.

John For the killing of my father, for the kidnapping of Lorna, I will not forgive thee, Doones.

All (*louder*) For the burning of our homes, for the ruin of our lives, For the terror in our hearts, we will not forgive thee, Doones.

Old John The time was good. A clear sky. The Doone men were in the mines. The women were alone. It could not have been better for us.

John Those are the houses. First, trap the men in the mines. Then we must bring the women and children out of the valley for safety. Then burn the houses. After, do what you want with the Doones. Now, I bid you spare the Counsellor, for Lorna's sake.

Fry Why, the Counsellor be the evilest of all, with his reasoning and guile. We hate him.

John Even so, I want him spared. I will kill no man, unless it be Carver himself, for I have a debt with him that no other man must honour.

Ridley Doone (*enters with a lantern*) Who goes there?

ALL (*shouting*) We will not forgive thee, Doones. (*they charge*)

*Ridley is shot. The **men** advance. Sounds of screaming and crying. Sky lit with flames of burning houses, smoke billowing. Chant continues.*

ALL For the plundering of our farms, the slaughter of our beasts, we will not forgive thee, Doones.
For the rape of our women, for the murder of our children, we will not forgive thee, Doones.
For the killing of my father, for the kidnapping of Lorna, We will not forgive thee, Doones.
For the burning of our homes, for the ruin of our lives, for the terror in our hearts, we will not forgive thee, Doones.

All freeze.

CARVER (*enters and shouts*) Do ye seek me, John Ridd? (*laughs, taunting, and goes.* **Men** *leave. The child,* **Ensie***, is alone, crying.* **John** *enters*)

JOHN Now don't be afraid, child. I'll look after you. What's your name?

ENSIE Ensie.

JOHN Ensie? After Sir Ensor, maybe? Who is your father?

ENSIE Carver is. Please don't send me back to him.

JOHN So you're the son of Carver Doone. His heir, no doubt. Well boy, you have risen out of the ashes of destruction. I never want to see again such a night of fire and slaughter and long-harboured revenge.

BOY (*enters*) It's all over. The Doones are dead.

JOHN Sir Ensor? And Carver?

BOY Vanished. But all the rest are dead. (*goes*)

John Then we have finished here. The Doones are vanquished. Come, Ensie. You're quite safe. You have a home with me now. (*goes with* **Ensie**)

The Ridd Household

Mrs. Ridd comes out to take **Ensie**. **John** *goes.*

Mrs. Ridd There child. We'll look after thee well. (*to audience*) A brave and wonderful thing has happened, and my John was at the lead of it. A night to be marvelled at and rejoiced over far and wide. The Doones have gone. And though my John wants nothing to do with the bloodshed and slaughter of that night, he was at the lead of it. He is the hero, make no mistake about that. And he is sent for by His Majesty the King. My John. (*goes with* **Ensie**)

Court of King James

Ceremonial music. **King James, The Queen, Lorna, courtiers** *enter.*

Queen You need your cloak, Lady Lorna. You are trembling. Are you unwell?

Lorna It is kind of your Majesty to notice, but I am quite well.

Courtier (*enters*) Your Majesty, Master John Ridd has arrived.

King Master Ridd? He is prompt. Show him in. (**John** *is presented, and bows low*) John Ridd, thou hast done great service to the realm, and to religion. You have rid the country of that great pestilence, the family of Doones. It was rare, it was rare, my lad. Now ask us anything in reason. What is thy chief ambition, lad?

John Well, my mother always used to think that having been schooled at Tiverton, I was worthy of a coat of arms. That is what she longs for.

61

King A good lad! A very good lad. And what is thy condition in life?

John I am a freeholder since the time of King Alfred. Our farm was a gift from him. We have had three very good harvests on the run and might support a coat of arms.

King You shall have a coat, my lad. But it will have to be a large one to fit you. And you shall have more, being such a loyal subject, and done such service. (**servant** *brings him cushion with sword on it*) Kneel, John Ridd. (**John** *kneels*. **King** *taps his shoulder with the sword*) Arise. Sir John Ridd! (**John** *stands up, astonished*)

John Sir, I be much obliged, but what be I to do with it?

Laughter. The **Queen** *places* **Lorna's** *hand in* **John's**.

Queen You have the King's blessing to marry Lady Dugal.

Lorna If you so wish, Sir John.

Peel of church bells, organ music. **King** *and* **Queen** *clap as* **John** *and* **Lorna**, *still hand in hand, process to church.* **Cast** *enter, singing, strewing flowers in front of the couple.* **Lizzie** *and* **Annie** *put a wedding veil on* **Lorna**, **Gwenny** *gives her a bouquet,* **Mrs. Ridd** *and* **Benita** *hug her and* **John**.

Benita My little lady Lorna.

Gwenny (*dabbing her eyes*) And girt Jan Ridd.

There is much cheering and laughter, then silence as **The priest** *enters.*

Priest Dearly beloved, we are gathered together here in the sight of God, and in the face of this congregation, to join together this man and this woman in holy matrimony.

Mrs. Ridd (*whispers*) Our John never looked so handsome!

Benita My Lorna never looked so beautiful.

Priest Sir John Ridd, wilt thou have this woman to be thy wedded wife, to live together after God's ordinance in the holy estate of matrimony? Wilt thou love her, comfort her, honour and keep her, in sickness and in health; and forsaking all others, keep thee only unto her, so long as ye both shall live?

John I will.

*While **Lorna** is making her vows, **Carver** flings open the door at back of church. He watches, unnoticed.*

Priest Lady Lorna Dugal, wilt thou have this man to be thy wedded husband, to live together after God's ordinance in the holy estate of matrimony? Wilt thou love him, comfort him, honour and keep him, in sickness and in health; and forsaking all others, keep thee only unto him, so long as ye both shall live?

Lorna I will.

***Priest** places **Lorna's** hand in **John's**. **Carver** steps forward to take **Ensie**, again unseen.*

John I, John Ridd, take thee, Lorna Dugal, to be my wedded wife, to have and to hold from this day forward, for better for worse, for richer for poorer, in sickness and in health, to love and to cherish, till death us do part, according to God's holy ordinance, and thereto I plight thee my troth.

Lorna I, Lorna Dugal, take thee, John Ridd, to be my wedded husband, to have and to hold from this day forward, for better for worse, for richer for poorer, in sickness and in health, to love, cherish and obey, till death us do part, according to God's holy ordinance, and thereto I plight thee my troth.

*As they exchange rings **Carver** raises a gun.*   73,75

Carver Take heed, John Ridd. Death has come to part thee.

He fires. **Lorna** *collapses in* **John's** *arms.* **People** *scream.*

John Lorna! She's dead! My wife is dead!

Carver *laughs, and goes with* **Ensie**.

All Imagine the terror, imagine the sorrow.

Men Blood on the altar steps, and she grows cold, so cold.

Women Her cheeks as pale as the white lilac blossom.

All The young husband stands with death in his arms.

John (*screams*) Carver Doone!

Annie, Lizzie and Gwenny *take* **Lorna** *from* **John**. *He goes.*

Women Imagine his flight over the dark moors.

Men Rain lashing down. Thunder rolling.

All Imagine him, mad with grief. The brutal deed, the piteous anguish, and cold despair. Imagine this. (*all go*)

Moors

Lightning flashing. Thunder. **Carver** *runs on with his cloak wrapped around* **Ensie**.

John (*offstage*) Carver Doone! Carver Doone! (*he enters*) Thy life or mine, Carver Doone, as the will of God may be. But we two live not one hour more together upon this earth.

Carver (*laughs, not turning*) You come unarmed, brave ploughboy. I have the gun I killed your Lorna with. I have the sword I killed your father with. Do you still challenge me? *(he turns to show that **Ensie** is inside his cloak.)*

ENSIE John, John! I'm frightened!

John *lifts up a branch.* ***Carver*** *fires, wounding* ***John***. ***John*** *swings with his branch and brings him down.* ***Ensie*** *runs to* ***John*** *and clings to him.*

JOHN Ensie, run. Run.

Ensie *runs off.* ***John*** *advances on* ***Carver*** *with his branch.*

CARVER I would not harm thee more, lad. I have punished you enough for your impertinence. You have been good and gracious to my little son. Go. I forgive thee.

JOHN I have no forgiveness left. (***John*** *presses the branch against* ***Carver*** *and slowly pins him to the ground,* ***Carver*** *struggles and then lies still, John stands.*) I will not harm thee any more. Carver Doone, thou art beaten. Own it, and thank God for it. Go thy way, and repent.*(goes)*

A flash of lightning. ***Carver*** *dies.*

OLD JOHN The bog closed around Carver Doone and took him out of this life. I went home with Ensie in my arms. I seemed to be riding in a dream. Only the thought of Lorna's death, like a heavy knell, was tolling in my brain.

The Ridd Household

John *staggers in, carrying* ***Ensie***. ***Mrs. Ridd*** *runs to help him.* ***Lizzie*** *takes* ***Ensie***.

MRS. RIDD God help you John. You're bleeding.

John Carver is dead. Let me see Lorna. Dead though she is, I want to see my wife.

Mrs. Ridd You must not see her yet.

John Not see her? Let me see my own dead one, and die.

Lizzie John, Annie is with her.

Mrs. Ridd John, listen to me. She lives! She lives!

Annie supports **Lorna** *and brings her to* **John's** *arms.* **Old John** *and* **Old Lorna** *come forward.*

Old Lorna Have you told our story well, John Ridd?

Old John I have nothing more to tell. Lorna is my life-long darling, and I love her more every day. She has given away her wealth, and with it, her past.

Old Lorna All that is done now. We are two simple people living our lives in the best way we can. Sometimes we think in humility of how our lives have changed from sorrow to joy. Read me our story, John.

Old John (*reading*) I, John Ridd of the parish of Oare, have seen and had some share in the doings of this neighbourhood, and will try to set them down. I intend to clear my parish from ill-fame.

All cast *come forward. Lights down*

THE END

Staging the play

In the notes on page 6, Berlie Doherty suggests two ways of staging *Lorna Doone*. One approach is to use a bare stage with no permanent set, and a minimum of props, which might include chairs and a table. Any props can be moved to different areas of the stage for different scenes. To help the audience follow the action and make sense of the play, characters such as Old John act as narrators (story-tellers), telling the audience where each scene takes place and who the key characters are. The rest is down to the actors' skill at creating characters and the atmospheres of different scenes. There might also be sound effects. The audience will need to use their imagination to supply the details they cannot see.

The other approach is to set up three acting areas on the stage. One area is for all the scenes in the Ridd household; one area represents Doone Valley and the interior of the Doones' house; the third area is used for all the other scenes, such as Judge Jeffrey's study, the inn and the court of King James. In this staging, there would be some kind of permanent set, although it could be very simple. An example of a possible set is shown below.

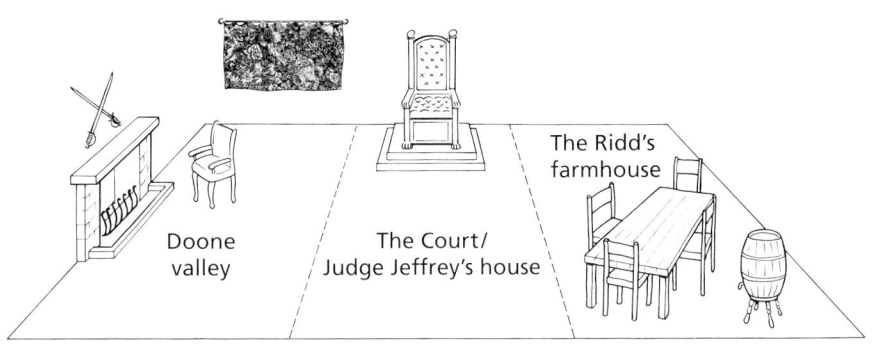

Stage set suggestion

In this design, the Ridd and Doone households are placed on opposite sides, and in opposite corners, of the stage. The outdoor scenes in Doone Valley take place in front (downstage) of the interior of the Doones' house. The Ridds' farmyard is the area upstage of the farmhouse kitchen. At the back of the stage, in the middle, is a large wooden chair, which is used as Judge Jeffrey's chair and King James's throne. Other scenes, for example, the inn scene, can take place at the front, in the middle of the stage.

Set design

In groups

A. The play is not divided into numbered scenes, because the action moves very quickly from one location to another. Go through the play and make a list of all the short sections, where each takes place, and their page numbers. Count the number of sections and check with other groups to see if they reach the same number. Discuss in your groups which of the two approaches to staging the play you like best. Note down your reasons, and share these with the rest of the class.

B. In the set diagram, a few articles of furniture have been included which might help to suggest the different atmospheres of the Doones' and Ridds' households. The swords and the tapestry, for example, are there to create mood – they are not used in the play. Make a list of items that would be easy to obtain which you could use instead of the additional props in the diagram. What moods are you trying to create with the props you use?

In groups

A. Design a set for a production of *Lorna Doone* that might take place in your school. Draw sketches of your ideas, showing the sets for the scenes – the Ridd household, the Doone Valley, the Doones' house, Judge Jeffrey's study and the court of King James. Experiment with different arrangements. Refer to the diagram on page 67 and think carefully about how the design may add to the drama of the play. In paired groups, share your designs explaining how you think your designs will work in performance.

You may find it helpful to draw a floor plan (to scale) of the space where you would put on the play, also considering where the audience will sit and how they will see the action.

B. Make a cardboard model of your set design.

MUSIC AND SOUND EFFECTS

Sound effects can convey information very simply and cheaply. Birdsong immediately tells the audience that they are watching an outdoor scene, probably in the countryside or a park; the choice of bird will affect the atmosphere created – think of the difference between a crow's voice and a blackbird's. Sound effects are also very useful for suggesting the weather: how many different weather sound effects can you think of?

Many local libraries have sound effects on tape and CD. You might even want to record your own for use in the performance.

Making sound effects

In groups

One interesting way of producing sound effects is to make 'live' sounds that are shown on stage as part of the performance. You can produce many different sounds with your voice, and hundreds more with musical instruments and other objects.

A. Choose three different locations (for example: a park, the seaside). Using your voices and whatever objects are available, create three sound effects that mimic well-known sounds you might hear in those places. When you are ready, ask the other groups to listen to the sound effects with their eyes shut, and then guess what sounds you are trying to mimic. You are not allowed to use any words in your sound effects.

Bear in mind that poor sound effects will undermine a production so it is important that they sound realistic.

B. Create a variety of live sound effects for:
- the first meeting of John and Lorna beneath the waterfall in Doone Valley — 12
- the attack on Doone Valley — 58–60
- the wedding procession — 62

C. Go through the play and decide which sound effects you will need for the different scenes, and how the effects will be achieved. Make only the effects as are necessary to help the audience imagine the scene for themselves.

You may well also want to include live or recorded music in your production. Try to develop a particular style for the show: choose music from one historical period for example, or make all the music yourselves. When you have decided on an approach, think of your decisions as the 'rules' of your production, and apply them to all questions of detail. For example, if you have decided to make your own music, don't then decide to mix it with recorded music for one moment in the play. If you stick to the rules you have made, your show will be much more powerful.

COSTUME

Lorna Doone is set in the late seventeenth century, and you may want to suggest this period in the costumes your actors wear. Providing a large cast with full period costumes can be expensive and difficult to achieve. Instead of this, you might want to dress the actors in 'neutral' costume, for example T-shirts and black trousers, and then use single items of period clothing to create the different characters.

> ### Costume design
>
> **As a class**
>
> Study the photographs from the 1934 film of *Lorna Doone* on pages 91–92. What are the key elements or details of the actors' costumes that suggest a particular period in history. Make a list of them. How might you achieve those costume effects simply, and for very little money?
>
> **In pairs**
>
> Write costume notes for the main characters in the play. Each character will need one or more special items of clothing, or props (for example, a walking stick or wicker basket), to suggest who they are. Different characters can use some of the same items, but in different combinations.

As with sound effects, your approach to costume will define the style of the production. You might want to keep all the costume items on stage on a clothes rail, with actors fetching the items they need when they want to 'put on' a character.

LIGHTING

If you are performing *Lorna Doone* in a theatre, you may be able to use stage lighting. This is very useful for defining areas on the stage, and marking scene changes, as well as creating the right atmosphere for different scenes. Before you decide how to use the stage lighting, go through the play and make notes on the scenes, noting down:

- where the scene takes place – indoors or outdoors?
- the time of day, and any details on the weather – bright or gloomy?
- the atmosphere of the scene – the Ridds' farmhouse has a different 'feel' to the Doones' hall.

Think carefully about how to achieve different lighting states for the indoor and outdoor scenes, and different times of day. Coloured gels (filters that are placed over the lens of the stage lights) can help define the mood of particular scenes. Set up an indoor scene, and, without moving any of the props, experiment with different kinds of lighting to create the atmosphere of the Doones' hall, then the Ridds' farmhouse.

Work on and around the script

Discussion

As a class

What are the key themes of *Lorna Doone*? Make a list of words that describe the events and emotions in the play. Here are two to start you off: love, revenge.

Drama

In groups

Choose a short scene from the play, and read it in your groups. Discuss what you think are the key themes of the scene, and what the feelings are of each character. Now devise a modern-day scene, with the same number of characters, and a similar story line. Will the modern-day characters behave in the same way? Perform the scene in front of the other groups, and ask them to guess which scene from *Lorna Doone* it was based on, and what the themes were that you identified. In what way does the present day treatment of the themes reveal differences between our society today, and that portrayed in *Lorna Doone*? How have the attitudes and perceptions of characters changed?

Discussion

As a class

Would it be possible to stage a 'modern' version of *Lorna Doone*? What fundamental changes would you make to the setting? Or is it only suitable for a costume drama?

Monologues

Lorna Doone is set in a world of sharp contrasts: between good and evil, romantic love and violent revenge. But the characters are not simply good or bad, saintly or wicked. For example, Sir Ensor Doone or Gwenny Carfax behave in ways that blur the edges between 'good' and 'bad' characters.

40
56

In pairs

Select a key incident in the play (for example: the death of John's father, Lorna's abduction, the attack on the Ridds' farm, John's arrival at King James's court) and choose two characters who were involved in the incident or were affected by it. Write two short monologues in which the characters reflect on the incident from their different points of view. Try to show the complicated mix of emotions that the characters feel. Perform the scenes, in character, first to each other, then to the rest of the class.

8–10
7, 49–50
61
44–45

On your own

Having written and listened to the monologues, you should have a clearer idea of the characters' motivations and reasons they behave in the way they do.

H

Referring to your monologues, rewrite the scene you have chosen as though it were a descriptive passage from the novel. As the narrator, make sure that you communicate the characters' feelings and their reactions to one another.

Newspaper story

On your own

A. Read the scene in the play in which Carver shoots Lorna at the wedding. Imagine you are a reporter from the local newspaper, *The Exmoor Eye*, sent to cover the story. Write an account of the event and its aftermath. The events will be confused, and the eye-witnesses will not all agree what took place. Your article will need an eye-catching headline.

63–4

H

B. As a reporter new to the area, you had never heard of Carver Doone and the infamous Doone family. Write a second article for the newspaper about the Doones, using as much information from the play as you can find. Your article will include accounts from the Doones' victims, and can include invented stories.

H

Legends and fairytales

Read the following extract, which is from R.D. Blackmore's preface to the novel *Lorna Doone*.

> The work is called a 'romance', because the incidents, characters, time, and scenery, are alike romantic … any son of Exmoor, chancing on this volume, cannot fail to bring to mind the nurse-tales of his childhood – the savage deeds of the outlaw Doones in the depths of Bagworthy Forest, the beauty of the hapless maid brought up in the midst of them, the plain John Ridd's Herculean power, and … the exploits of Tom Faggus.

As a class

A. 'Romantic' does not only mean 'sentimental' or 'lovey-dovey'. What else does the word mean? Which scenes in the play do you think are romantic, and why?

B. Find some examples of plays, films or books that you would describe as romantic. What makes a good romance? Using the examples you have found, can you find features that they have in common? Is there is a formula for writing romance?

On your own

A. Blackmore compares *Lorna Doone* to a fairytale. Can you think of any fairytales that scenes in the play remind you of? Find a collection of fairytales, and read some examples, looking for themes that appear in *Lorna Doone*.

B. Traditionally, fairytales and legends were not written down. Each generation of story-tellers would memorise the stories their parents had told them when they were children. Choose one of the stories you have read and think about the opening episode. Now create a picture of the episode in your imagination. Try to see the characters and their actions as if you were watching a film, perhaps in slow motion so you can see all the detail. Now invent a start to your story that will 'capture' your listener.

As a class

You should now know the beginning of your stories well enough to be able to tell them in your own words. In pairs as storytellers, tell each other

cont…

the opening episode. Afterwards, talk about how each story worked – did the listener want to hear what happened next? Could the telling be made more dramatic? If so, how? Now change partners and retell the stories. Was the second telling different?

Discussion

With each retelling of the stories, it is likely that changes will have been introduced, although the basic story (framework) will have remained the same. How many different types of story can you think of that follow a set pattern and end in a way you could have predicted at the beginning? For example, do you expect the bad characters to triumph in fairy tales? Think of books you have read as well as TV programmes, films and plays you have seen.

Writing letters and diary entries

On your own

A. EITHER Imagine that Lorna keeps a secret diary that is never shown to anyone. Write a series of entries in the diary, written during the months when John is away in London. Invent small events in her daily life, and try to suggest how her mood changes from day to day, in the way she writes in the diary. The last entry can be for the day in which she finally sees John again.

H

20–29

OR Carver Doone knows that he might be killed himself when he attacks Lorna at the wedding. Imagine that he writes a letter to his son, Ensie, in the week before the wedding, trying to explain his actions. He will add new thoughts each day. Write this letter, trying to suggest, in his series of entries in the letter, the state of mind that would lead him to the attempted murder. Is he a cold-blooded killer, or has he gone insane?

63–4

B. Gwenny Carfax keeps the letters John sends to Lorna while she is staying at her uncle's house, and doesn't show them to her mistress. Write extracts from these letters, showing how John begins to despair of seeing her again.

56

H

The life and times of R. D. Blackmore

> "I was launched into this vale of tears on the 7th of June 1825, at Longworth in Berkshire. Before I was four months old, my mother was taken to a better world, and so I started crookedly."
>
> R. D. Blackmore

Richard Doddridge Blackmore did not have an easy start to life. His mother and sister died in a typhus outbreak when he was only a baby, and he was then brought up by relatives. Richard's father, John Blackmore, was a poor clergyman. The family was reunited in 1831, when John Blackmore remarried and brought his children home to his new parish in Devon. From then on, all of Richard's childhood was spent in the West Country, which took a strong hold on him. His love for Devon, which he described as his "almost native land", comes over very clearly in *Lorna Doone*.

When he was eleven, Richard was sent to Blundell's School in Tiverton, Devon, the same school from which John Ridd is fetched at the beginning of the novel. It was a rough boarding school, but Richard was not unhappy there. He went on to study Classics at Exeter College, Oxford, where he was known as a good scholar.

After university he studied law, and became a barrister in London in 1852. It was not to last. After only six years, he was forced to give up his career, after developing epilepsy. He wrote: "My medical adviser said I would have to give up my profession, seek an outdoor employment, or die young."

He did not regret leaving the law, as it allowed him to pursue his real ambition, to become a writer. But it was not easy. His first book of poems, published in 1854, got poor reviews and sold very few copies, and his next few books did not do much better. Luckily, three years later, he inherited some money from his uncle, and he was able to set himself up in business as a fruit grower in Teddington. For the rest of his life, R.D. Blackmore divided his time between growing fruit and writing; the eventual success of his novels helped to pay his debts as a fruit-grower – the business never made him any money!

R.D. Blackmore was a very private man – even his neighbours did not know much about him. A long-time customer of his wrote: "He is not a social man, and seems wedded to his garden in summer, and his book-writing in winter ... he keeps the most vicious dogs to protect his fruit, and I would advise you to avoid the risk of visiting him."

In 1853 Blackmore married Lucy Maguire, a Roman Catholic, a fact which he kept secret for years from his father. She was often ill, and became a semi-invalid, so that Blackmore spent much of his time looking after her. They were never to have any children. Blackmore's own health was poor, and it cannot have been an easy life, but his few intimate friends remembered him as always in good spirits.

Blackmore's first novel, *Clara Vaughan*, appeared in 1864, but it was not successful. Finally, in 1869, *Lorna Doone* was published, and Blackmore's luck turned: it was an instant public and critical success. In the next ten years, it sold thousands of copies, and has never been out-of-print since.

Blackmore continued to write for the rest of his life, publishing 15 novels, which were mostly better received by the public than by the critics. It is for *Lorna Doone* that he is now best remembered. R.D. Blackmore died in 1900.

R.D. Blackmore

Exmoor Legends

As a child living in Devon, Blackmore was told stories about Exmoor and the legendary Doone family, which gave him ideas for many of the episodes in the novel. Exmoor had a reputation as a remote and lawless place, and there are many local tales of cattle thieves and murderous gangs. No one knows for sure whether the Doones ever actually existed, but they must have seemed real enough to the young Richard. A typical story, which an old Exmoor lady remembered being told when she was a child in the 1850s, went as follows:

…I remember my grandmother telling me of a terrible robbery at Badgeworthy. She said: "After they were gone to bed, robbers came and kicked the bullocks with pricks (prikes) and made them roar. The master sent the foreman down to see what was the matter with them. When he went down the robbers killed him. Then the bullocks began to roar again, then another went down – they served him the same. They began to roar again, then the master went down in a rage and they killed him. The little boy heard the robbers coming. He crept into a hole in the chimney … When they went upstairs they could only find the baby. They then took what they wanted and went off. The next day the neighbours were told about it and a great dog came and licked up the blood, and they flung a chopping-hook at him and made him bleed, and they traced the blood to the place where the robbers were, and they were all taken."

Discussion

As a class

Writers often use events in their own lives as material for their novels. Compare the biography of R.D. Blackmore and the old woman's story, above, with the themes and events of the play. Can you find examples of ways in which Blackmore's own life might have influenced the writing of Lorna Doone?

Writing

On your own.

H

EITHER Write a short story about people living in a wild and remote part of the countryside (perhaps somewhere you have visited, or read about). Set the story in a particular period in history. Picture the lives your characters might lead, think of a book you have read or a historical film you have seen, and borrow some of the details to give a sense of the period in which your story is set.

cont...

OR Imagine you are a traveller in 17th century Devon who is used to living in a town or city. Write a story or a series of diary extracts describing the sights you see and the people you meet. How do the local people react to you? Do you run into any trouble? Do you find the area beautiful or threatening? You could use characters and scenes from the novel or play as inspiration.

OR Choose a story from the area in which you live, perhaps based on a character or an event that people like to talk about. Think about how much the story might be developed to make it more interesting. You do not have to be true to the original in every detail; your imagination is free to make what it likes of the story. So for example, you may wish to add new events or characters or exaggerate some aspects of the tale to make them more intriguing. In this way, you can take ownership of a well-known story. When you do this, you are more likely to interest your listener or reader.

From novel to playscript

Read the extract from the novel, below, which describes the attack on Doone Valley.

The moon was lifting well above the shoulder of the uplands, when we, the chosen band, set forth … we were not to begin our climbing until we heard a musket fired from the heights, on the left hand side, where John Fry himself was stationed, upon his own and his wife's request, to keep him out of combat … John Fry was to fire his gun, with a ball of wool inside it, so soon as he heard the hurly-burly at the Doone-gate beginning; which we, by reason of waterfall, could not hear, down in the meadows there.

We waited a very long time, with the moon marching up heaven steadfastly, and the white fog trembling in chords and quavers, like a silver harp on the meadows. And then the moon drew up the fogs, and scarfed herself in white with them; and so being proud, gleamed upon the water, like a bride at her looking-glass; and yet there was no sound of either John Fry or his blunderbuss.

…suddenly the most awful noise that anything short of thunder could make, came down among the rocks, and went and hung upon the corners.

'The signal, my lads!' I cried, leaping up, and rubbing my eyes … 'Now hold on by the rope, and lay your quarter-staffs across, my lads and keep your guns pointing to heaven, lest haply we shoot one another.'

'Us shan't never shutt one another, wi' our goons at that mark, I reckon,' said an oldish chap, but as tough as leather, and esteemed a wit for his dryness.

'You come next to me, old Ike; you be enough to dry up the waters: now remember, all lean well forward. If any man throws his weight back, down he goes; and perhaps he may never get up again; and most likely he will shoot himself.'

… However, though a gun went off, no one was any the worse for it, neither did the Doones notice it, in the thick of the firing in front of them. For the order to those of the sham attack, conducted by Tom Faggus, was to make the greatest possible noise, without exposure of themselves; until we, in the rear, had fallen to; which John Fry was again to give the signal of.

Therefore we, of the chosen band, stole up the meadow quietly, keeping in the blots of shade, and the hollow of the watercourse. And the earliest notice the Counsellor had, or any one else, of our presence, was the blazing of the logwood house, where lived that villain Carver. It was my especial privilege to set this house on fire; upon which I had insisted, exclusively and conclusively. No other hand but mine should lay a brand, or strike steel on flint for it; I had made all preparations carefully for a good blaze. And I must confess that I rubbed my hands, with a strong delight and comfort, when I saw the home of that man, who had fired so many houses, having its turn of smoke, and blaze, and of crackling fury.

We took good care, however, to burn no innocent women, or children, in that most righteous destruction. For we brought them all out beforehand; some were glad and some were sorry; according to their dispositions. For Carver had ten or a dozen wives; and perhaps that had something to do with his taking the loss of Lorna so easily. One child I noticed, as I saved him; a fair and handsome little fellow, beloved by Carver Doone, as much as any thing beyond himself could be. The boy climbed on my back, and rode; and much as I hated his father, it was not in my heart to say, or do, a thing to vex him.

… In the smoke, and rush, and fire, they believed that we were a hundred; and away they ran, in consternation, to the battle of the Doone-gate.

'All Doone-town is on fire, on fire!' we heard them shrieking as they went: 'a hundred soldiers are burning it, with a dreadful great man at the head of them!'

Discussion

As a class

58–61

Compare this account of the battle with the version in the play, noting the differences. What key events are missed out in the play?

- Why do you think the story has been simplified?
- What techniques does Berlie Doherty use to create the atmosphere of the battle?
- Do you think the play version is effective? Give reasons.

Writing

On your own.

H

A. Write your own stage version of the attack on Doone Valley, based on the passage above. You may want to read the chapter 'A Long Account Settled', from which the extract is taken. Before you write the scene, think about the different 'devices' you might want to use to tell the story, and create the right atmosphere: dialogue, narrative (story-telling), stage directions. The scene can include as many characters as you want. Think also about the language you use: will you try to recreate the West Country dialect (local way of speaking) that Old Ike uses in the extract? In the play Berlie Doherty uses a kind of rhythmic verse to create a tense, battle-like atmosphere. There are many different ways to write the scene – try to make your scene both original and memorable.

B. Imagine you are a newspaper reporter who has gone with John Ridd's band on the night of the attack. Write a newspaper report of the events for the front page of your newspaper including:

H
- a headline
- eyewitness accounts
- a description of the scene, both on the night and the following morning
- a brief explanation of why the attack has taken place.

Themes in and around the play

THE MONMOUTH REBELLION AND THE BLOODY ASSIZES

The Duke of Monmouth

Jeremy Stickles, on page 36 of the play, tells John in private the reason why he has come to the West Country. He has come, he says, 'to watch the hatching of a secret plot …'. *Lorna Doone* is set in the second half of the seventeenth century, and the 'secret plot' is a real historical event: the Duke of Monmouth's rebellion against King James II.

Monmouth's Rising

The seventeenth century in England was a period of great uncertainty and upheaval. England had suffered a Civil War, when parliament rebelled against King Charles I after years of warfare and heavy taxation. Charles I had been executed; there had been a ten-year republic, and then the restoration of the monarchy, with King Charles II in 1660. The years that followed were marked by wars and shifting alliances in Europe, and rivalry and political intrigue in England.

The greatest cause of conflict was religion. Most English people were Protestants, and bitterly opposed to Roman Catholicism. Charles II, however, though not a Catholic himself, was greatly attracted to Catholicism. As he lay dying, in February 1685, he had the satisfaction of knowing that he would be succeeded by a Catholic on the throne. Since Charles II had no legitimate son, the throne would pass to his brother James, the Duke of York. For James, Catholicism was the true faith, and he meant to re-establish it in England once he became king.

The Duke of Monmouth entering Lyme Regis with 1500 men

Many people could not accept the idea of a Catholic king. Looking for a Protestant alternative, they turned to the Duke of Monmouth, who was Charles II's illegitimate son. Charles had been very fond of Monmouth, and made him one of the leading members of the Court. Monmouth had also held high commands in the Army, and was a respected soldier. Some supporters of the Duke tried to pretend that he was, in fact, legitimate, spreading a story that Charles II had secretly married Monmouth's mother.

In 1682, Monmouth fled to Holland, after a plot against King Charles and the Duke of York was discovered. With Charles's death, in February 1685, and the Duke of York's coronation as King James II, it looked as if Monmouth's hopes of becoming king were doomed. But his supporters did not give up hope. They encouraged him to believe that if he returned to England and led a rebellion against the new king, England would rise in support of Monmouth's claim to the throne. The Duke allowed himself to be convinced by their optimism.

Monmouth landed at Lyme Regis in Dorset, in May 1685. At first the signs were encouraging. Many ordinary people rallied in support of his cause, and he was greeted as a hero when, in Taunton, he took the bold move of declaring himself king. Crucially, however, the powerful aristocracy failed to support him, preferring to wait and see what happened. While Monmouth toured the West Country in search of men and money to fight King James, James's loyal commanders assembled an army to confront the rebels.

The Battle of Sedgemoor

Engraving of the Battle of Sedgemoor, 6 July 1685

The battle took place near Bridgwater in Somerset. Monmouth's army was smaller and less professional than the Royalist forces, but the Duke decided he had to risk an attack, or lose his last chance of success. He decided on the desperate plan of leading his peasant army in a night attack on the Royalist right flank, an operation that would have been difficult even for highly trained troops. Monmouth led his men over the open moor in complete darkness, but a pistol shot alerted the Royalist guards to their approach. A sentry shouted,

'For whom are you?'
'For the King!' the rebels shouted back.
'For *which* King?'
'For King Monmouth, and God with us!'

They were answered by a volley of musket fire. With the element of surprise lost, Monmouth had no chance of winning the battle, and as an experienced commander he knew it. For some time he attempted to encourage his men, but when the opposing cavalry charged, Monmouth mounted his horse and fled. By morning, with the rebel army routed and in full retreat, Monmouth's rebellion and the last battle to be fought on English soil were over.

Macaulay's account

In groups

R.D. Blackmore based his version of the events of 1685 on the account by the historian Thomas Macaulay. Read the extract below, which tells the story of the aftermath of the Battle of Sedgemoor.

> It was four o'clock: the sun was rising; and the routed army came pouring into the streets of Bridgewater. The uproar, the blood, the gashes, the ghastly figures which sank down and never rose again, spread horror and dismay through the town. The pursuers, too, were close behind. Those inhabitants who had favoured the insurrection expected sack and massacre, and implored the protection of their neighbours who professed the Roman Catholic religion … During that day the conquerors continued to chase the fugitives. The neighbouring villagers long remembered with what a clatter of horsehoofs and what a storm of curses the whirlwind of cavalry swept by. Before evening five hundred prisoners had been crowded into the parish church of Weston Zoyland. Eighty of them were wounded; and five expired within the consecrated walls. Great numbers of labourers were impressed for the purpose of burying the slain. A few, who were notoriously partial to the vanquished side, were
>
> *cont…*

set apart for the hideous office of quartering the captives. The tithing men of the neighbouring parishes were busied in setting up gibbets and providing chains. All this while the bells of Weston Zoyland and Chedzoy rang joyously, and the soldiers sang and rioted on the moor amidst the corpses. For the farmers of the neighbourhood had made haste, as soon as the event of the fight was known, to send hogsheads of their best cider as peace offerings to the victors.

A. The extract above includes some words which may be unfamiliar, and the meaning of some sentences may be unclear. Using a good dictionary, such as the *Collins Millennium English Dictionary*, go through the passage and try to unravel all the meanings. Make brief notes on all the events Macaulay describes.

Criminal court

Using the extract, note down some of the crimes that might have taken place around Bridgwater on the day after the battle. Imagine you are modern-day police officers interviewing an imaginary citizen of Bridgwater who witnessed the events described in the extract. In groups, write the notes from the police interview. Create an identity for the witness — their sex, name, age, occupation, and personality — before you begin to write the notes.

As a class

Some citizens of Bridgwater are later taken to court for looting, and drunken behaviour. Set up an imaginary court to try them for their crimes. You will need to decide:
- who the defendants (accused people) are — create names and characters for them, and choose people to play them in the trial
- the charges — what they are accused of

From the class, select:
- a judge, to oversee the proceedings
- a team of lawyers for the defence
- a team of lawyers for the prosecution
- witnesses for the defence and prosecution — use some of the witness statements from the police interviews
- a jury

cont...

Each of the witnesses will need to have a clear identity, and a story to tell. Make notes for all witnesses before the trial begins. Decide on how the trial will be conducted, and the order in which the witnesses will appear. At the end of the trial, the jury will discuss and agree verdicts on the different charges. If there are guilty verdicts, the judge will decide on the sentence.

The Bloody Assizes

Look at the two documents below. What do you think they are?

After the Monmouth Rebellion was over, the defeated rebels were punished very severely. King James sent the country's leading judge, Lord Chief Justice Jeffreys, to the West Country to deliver justice. The trials that followed became known as The Bloody Assizes.

One Pitts is to be Whipt through every Town in Dorsetshire for Seaven Years togeather

Prisoners Executed at Exeter for High Treason

John Floweracres
Thomas Hobbs
John Oliver
Henry Knight
Samuell Pores
John Knowles
William Parsons
Thomas Quinton
Thomas Broughton
John Gosling
John Sprake
William Clegg
John Rosse
Timothy Dunkin

Prisoners to bee transported for high Treason for whome a Warrant is delivered

Jerome Nipho
Graham Hunt
Christopher Cooper
(illegible) Brevett
(illegible) Follett
(illegible) Kemplyn
(illegible) Rape

Edward Merrick in Wells Goale to bee transported in the place of Walter Reaps

Television documentary

In groups

Using your local library and the internet, find out everything you can about the Monmouth rebellion, Judge Jeffreys and the Bloody Assizes. Choose one aspect that you find particularly interesting and put together a presentation in the form of a TV documentary on events relating to the Monmouth rebellion and aftermath.

Your documentaries should be no longer than five minutes in length and should be both interesting and informative. You should also be able to explain why you have chosen to focus on your specific subject matter – against the historical context.

You might include short scenes, in which actors play the roles of different historical characters. There could also be interviews with experts, visual materials (for example: maps, paintings and photographs) and a spoken narrative (the telling of the story).

CLASS IN VICTORIAN ENGLAND

Lorna Doone is set in the seventeenth century, but it was written by a nineteenth century author. How the characters behave might tell us something about Victorian attitudes to class and social status, and to the role of women in society.

Discussion

As a class

- Lorna is one of the central characters in the play but she is rarely (if ever) allowed to do as she pleases. Do you agree that it is the men in *Lorna Doone* who have all the power, while the women do as they are told?
- If you think of the society of *Lorna Doone* as a pyramid with the king at the top, where in the pyramid do the different characters fit? Who has a higher social status than who? Draw a large pyramid on the board, and add the names of the characters to it. Do you all agree who belongs where?

cont...

- Can you find any evidence to suggest whether the author of *Lorna Doone* supports or rejects this traditional class system? How are the characters of different classes represented?
- Is there a class system in our own society? How have things changed since Victorian times?

A Victorian Lorna Doone

In the play, John Ridd is concerned about how Lorna will take to being a farmer's wife. Until the nineteenth century, a farmer's wife would be expected to take a very active part in the running of the farm. She would manage the dairy, making butter and cheese, look after poultry and bake bread, as well as raising the family – an average of seven children. On top of that she might have to cook, both for the family and the farmhands. Even the more prosperous farmer's wives, who might employ domestic servants, would expect to work very hard.

In the Victorian age, as farming became more profitable and social attitudes changed, women were discouraged from carrying out many of these traditional tasks. Wealthier farmers' wives were no longer expected to have any contact with farm labourers; farm dairies were replaced by industrial manufacture; domestic work was held to be unladylike. Instead of farm-work, women were supposed to devote themselves to suitably feminine activities, such as attending church, needlework and playing the piano. Farmers' wives, like middle-class women in the cities, were responsible for keeping up appearances. Cornelius Stovin, a farmer, wrote in the 1870s about his wife, Lizzie:

"She is fond of a vase and understands the adornments of a home…I notice a great change towards a loftier and more refined civilization hallowing our dwellings which had not taken place during my childhood."

Lizzie even refused to bake bread, though the farm was in debt and she knew how to bake.

Women who did work as farmers, either through choice or necessity, found their lives made doubly difficult by the attitudes of farming society. In *Far From the Madding Crowd* by Thomas Hardy, the heroine, Bathsheba Everdene, tries to farm a property she has inherited. In her first visit to the Corn Market, the local farmers make their feelings clear.

Among these heavy yeomen, a feminine figure glided, the single one of her sex that the room contained. She was prettily and even daintily dressed. She moved between them as a chaise between carts … was felt among them like a breeze among furnaces. It had required a little determination – far more than she at first imagined – to take up a position there, for at her first entry, the lumbering dialogues had ceased, nearly every face had been turned towards her and those that were already turned rigidly fixed there.

Writing

On your own.

Imagine how Bathsheba feels, with all the men's eyes on her. Have you ever been unwillingly the centre of attention in a group of people? Write a story in which a newcomer to a town or village is made to feel unwelcome by the people who live there. Write from the point of view of the newcomer.

H

Media

Read the extract overleaf, which is from the film script of the 1934 film.

Still from the film

cont...

Still from the film

LORNA DOONE

The MAIN and CREDIT TITLES appear in old English script on the pages of a vellum book, which turn to show each title in order. The page following the Credits bears the words, in the same script:

> IN THE YEAR OF OUR LORD 1673,
> THE DOONES, AN OUTLAW CLAN OF
> NOBLE LINEAGE, LIVED SECURE IN
> THEIR STRONGHOLD ON THE WILDS OF
> EXMOOR.

A hand with a quill pen is writing the last word.
During this title the MUSIC of the DOONE motif is heard and carries over as we

DISSOLVE TO:

WILD EXMOOR SKYLINE
...a dark silhouette of a hillside, on which is moving downwards a single file of horsemen, dark figures against an angry sky. The impression is of a grim and purposeful descent of angry men.

This is the sombre background for the following title:

> RUTHLESS AND ARROGANT, THE DOONES
> PREYED UPON A PEACEFUL COUNTRYSIDE.

The figures of the horsemen (seen in MEDIUM LONG SHOT) are still passing in their unbroken line as we –
FADE OUT.

(End of titles)

SEQUENCE "A"

A-1 MOORLAND – AND FLOCK OF SHEEP – DAY
     With shepherds, slowly moving across the moor.
                                                    (MUSIC)

     DISSOLVE TO:

A-2 MOORLAND – BESIDE THE SEA
     A pictorial shot of a beautiful sunny landscape, with a glimpse of the sea.
                                                    (MUSIC)

     CUT TO:

A-3 GULLS
     ...wheeling slowly in the sky.
                                                    (MUSIC)

     CUT TO:

A-4 GORSE BUSH
     ...in flower, if possible. A gun barrel protrudes from the bush, swings into CAMERA
                                                    (MUSIC)

     and is fired
     CUT TO:

A-5 GULLS
     ...scattering with wild cries
     (A FLASH)
                                                    (MUSIC)

     CUT TO:

A-6 GIBBET ON MOOR – DAY
     FULL SHOT
     ...on a horse saddled but riderless, plunging and galloping away. We are near a rough road which passes near the gibbet.
                                                                    (MUSIC)
     DISSOLVE TO:

A-7 COURTYARD PLOVER BARROW – EXT – DAY
     FULL SHOT
     ...on yard, with the same horse galloping into the courtyard. A man near the gate gives a cry.
                              MAN
                         Mistress Ridd!
                         Mistress Ridd!
     People come running. MISTRESS RIDD, followed by servant BETTY MUXWORTHY, appears at the kitchen door. JOHN FRY runs in from barn door and catches the horse.
                                                                    (MUSIC)
     CUT TO:

A-8 FULL SHOT ON MISTRESS RIDD
     CAMERA shooting past horse, which JOHN FRY is holding, as MISTRESS RIDD comes in from kitchen door. She touches the horse's wither and finds her hand stained with blood.

Discussion

As a class

The extract is from the opening pages of the film's shooting script – this is the script the director uses to make the film, including directions for the different camera shots and music. There is very little dialogue in the extract, but a lot of information is conveyed.

- List, in detail, all the elements of the plot of *Lorna Doone* that are contained in the extract.
- What devices (such as dialogue, music) does the extract use to tell the story?
- How long do you think the extract would be in the finished film?
- How much of the story would a viewer who speaks no English understand at this point?

✍ Write a film script

On your own

Choose a short section of the play which includes action but does not require very much dialogue. Using the extract as a guide, write a shooting script for a sequence which might last only 30 seconds, but which includes changes of camera angle and strong visual images. Write in the same format as the extract, including some of the film-making terms that are used there.

Research resources and further reading

R.D. Blackmore
R.D. Blackmore by WH Dunn [*out of print*]
The Last Victorian by KG Budd [*out of print*]

The Monmouth Rebellion
A Monarchy Transformed: Britain 1603–1714 by Mark Kishlansky (Penguin)
The Monmouth Rebellion and the Bloody Assizes (Jackdaw, No. 34)
The History of England by Thomas Babington Macaulay (Penguin Classics)

Further reading
Lorna Doone by R.D. Blackmore
Far from the Madding Crowd by Thomas Hardy